MODERN HUMANITIES RESEARC.
NEW TRANSLATIONS
VOLUME 12

GENERAL EDITOR
ALISON FINCH

GERMANIC EDITOR
RITCHIE ROBERTSON

HUGO VON HOFMANNSTHAL
An Impossible Man

TRANSLATED BY WITH AN INTRODUCTION BY
ALEXANDER STILLMARK

Hugo von Hofmannsthal

An Impossible Man

Translated with an Introduction by
Alexander Stillmark

Modern Humanities Research Association
2016

Published by

The Modern Humanities Research Association,
Salisbury House
Station Road
Cambridge CB1 2LA
United Kingdom

First published 2016

ISBN 978-1-78188-274-0

www.translations.mhra.org.uk

CONTENTS

ACKNOWLEDGEMENTS

My sincere thanks are due to Ritchie Robertson for his astute and invariably helpful scrutiny of my translation; also to Timothy Lumsdaine for his expertise in establishing the layout of the text.

INTRODUCTION

Depth must be concealed. Where?
On the surface. (Hofmannsthal)

I

George Meredith, in his masterly, wide-ranging *Essay on Comedy* (1877), offers us a definition of social comedy which is particularly apposite to Hofmannsthal's achievement as comic playwright:

> The laughter of Comedy is impersonal and of unrivalled politeness, nearer a smile; often no more than a smile. It laughs through the mind, for the mind directs it; and it might be called the humour of the mind.

Hofmannsthal himself, widely versed as he was in the European literary tradition, greatly valued Meredith's essay and would certainly have concurred with its conclusion that 'the test of true Comedy is that it shall awaken thoughtful laughter.' For the comedies he left to posterity, from the early Casanova studies (*The Adventurer and the Singer, Christina's Homeward Journey*) through the *Rosenkavalier* down to the late comedies with their contemporary settings (*An Impossible Man, The Incorruptible Servant*), are all distinguished by a high degree of verbal sophistication. The broader effects of buffoonery and caricature, comic distortion or drastic emphasis, were neither to his taste nor did they come naturally to his subtler talent, as his contentious correspondence with the far robuster Richard Strauss clearly bears out. The comic libretti he wrote for the composer, so celebrated today, in fact constitute a hard-gained compromise: the successful result of a difficult collaboration between two disparate artistic temperaments whose notions of comedy often stood far apart. Unlike Strauss, Hofmannsthal was not attracted to burlesque or tomfoolery on the stage; his view of comedy is essentially rooted in the refinements of irony. The finer points of ambiguity, antithetical relations, subtle juxtaposition and contrast, are valued by him far beyond the brasher effects of farce. He chooses wit rather than waggishness, pregnant silences rather than startling stunts. Being above all a poet with a fine ear for verbal nuance, Hofmannsthal developed his comic dialogue as a high literary art, having learnt his lesson from major models like Molière, Goldoni, Shakespeare or Lessing, but also from past masters within the tradition of Viennese popular comedy. A vast collection of occasional jottings, notes and observations bear witness to this tireless study of classics in the genre. The uses of Hofmannsthal's comedic language are, as will be seen, refined and complex. He worked at the the text over more than ten years, revising and condensing his material in order to achieve the desired formal balance and clarity. As for the human image projected by his comic theatre, this is consistently and eminently paradoxical. Mankind is seen as an endless mass of comic contradiction. Of course, there is nothing strikingly new about that: all important writers of comedy since Aristophanes have worked in similar vein to expose to ridicule the unresolved, contrary human enigma. Yet there is something quite distinctive (and one is inclined to say, peculiarly Austrian) in the way Hofmannsthal naturally combines the established features and formulas of tradition with the vernacular accents of a familiar world, received and mediated by a modern sensibility. Being a native of Vienna and heir to its richly cosmopolitan heritage, he was acutely sensitive to the coexistence, within its culture, of disparate elements; a compound of past and present, a contrast of ties and breaks in tradition. As he once expressed it in a late public speech entitled 'The Legacy of Antiquity' (1926): 'The Old and the New is present side by side, it is truly somewhat more present for us than it is elsewhere.' The fact that he chose to represent this wealth of contrast and contradiction by symbolic means, above all through the medium of pervasive irony, and not in the style of the Naturalists, lent his contributions to the comic genre their distinctive polish and poise.

II

Few European writers of the *fin de siècle* could claim to rival in breadth and diversity of talent the Austrian poet Hugo von Hofmannsthal (1874–1929). Born in Vienna, and only son to Hugo Laurenz August Hofmann, Edler von Hofmannsthal, and his wife Anna (nee Fohleutner), he enjoyed most of the benefits and privileges of the well-to-do middle classes, attending the 'Akademisches Gymnasium' and receiving thorough grounding in both classical and modern languages. A prodigious reader from an early age, he began publishing lyric poetry from his sixteenth year under the pseudonym of 'Loris' and rose to immediate fame and acceptance among the literati of Young Vienna (which included Hermann Bahr, Arthur Schnitzler, Felix Salten, Richard Beer-Hofmann, PeterAltenberg) before he had even left school. Steeped as he was in the European literary tradition, he diversified his protean gifts into many forms as he matured, moving away from the early poetry and lyrical drama, to the libretto, short story, novel and essay, whilst broadening his range to anthologist, reviver of the medieval mystery play, tragedian and comic playwright. His collaboration with Richard Strauss in the years which began with *Elektra* (1906) and lasted to the year of his death in 1929 made him into a household name on the opera stage. Similarly, his enduring friendship with Max Reinhardt proved most fruitful for the theatre, not least in bringing into being the Salzburg Festival (1911). Hofmannsthal was intuitively conscious of an organic process, within himself, of growth and development, which he attempted to trace out in later life in schematic annotations entitled *ad me ipsum*. This cryptic self-appraisal was to serve the enquiring reader as a basic guide to the progressive stages of the playwright's development. Hofmannsthal early felt a particular affinity with the Goethean idea of a secret unity underlying most natural and human phenomena, which he expressed in the following terms:

As a young man I perceived the unity of the world, the religious idea, in its beauty; the manifold beauty of all beings moved me, the contrasts, and the fact that all of them actually related to one another. Later it was the separate entity and the forces at work behind this lovely unity which I felt impelled to represent; yet I never abandoned that sense of unity. (March 1922)

A significant part of this notion of a fundamental coherence in his maturation as playwright also relates to his approach to comic theatre. He increasingly came to see the comedy as the fullest possible embodiment of the social idea. Indeed, he explicitly called his concept of comedy 'the achieved idea of the social'. His earliest playlets of the eighteen-nineties were lyrical in style and filled with that alluring symbolism which was prevalent in the age of aestheticism, though tempered by a distinctive ethical accentuation that set them apart. Hofmannsthal's first full-scale comedy, *Christina's Homeward Journey* (1909), like his *Rosenkalier* (1910), is given a fanciful Rococo setting, being transported, as it were, into an impressionistic, rarified substitute reality at some remove from the harsher world of common experience. It took Hofmannsthal several determined steps to reach a premise which embraced the contemporary world, to create more sharply defined figures belonging to that world, and an appropriate vernacular language imbued with critical edge.

The influences upon the playwright in attaining to his rather abstract notion of social comedy are varied and complex. Within the German context, it was Lessing's *Minna von Barnhelm* (1767) which offered him the most enduring model. This too was a comedy set in the immediate aftermath of war; it was no less concerned with a love intrigue involving a diffident, vacillating hero and a spirited young heroine, very much his equal, who could manipulate her lover. It was based on clearly defined social stratification, rich in ironic inconsistensies, finely tuned in the dialogue registers to produce contrastive effects. Above all it was a lucid construct of classical elegance, in which the shifting configuration of characters was handled with admirable precision. Hofmannsthal was inherently attracted to the well-made play. He once wrote that in comedy 'Lessing is a master of the indirect'. And it was this essential trait which he also identified in Molière: 'In the *Misanthrope* the entire dialogue is criticism from beginning to end'; to which he adds in elaboration: 'criticism is only one form of the indirect.' Hofmannsthal studied Molière closely from his earliest preoccupation with the comedy and the benefits he derived from such critical scrutiny can hardly be overestimated. The art of creating dramatic constellations, grouping figures to produce tense confrontations, the difficult art of keeping scenes 'pure' or uncluttered, the subtle interplay between high and low modes of language, the art of sustaining the energy of comedic dialogue, are some of the important insights he gained through his perusal of the grand master. It can hardly be overlooked that Alceste shares a certain family likeness with Hans Karl, even if the latter is more distrustful of the uses of language than of humankind.

Another important point of reference is the tradition of light Viennese social comedy (Konversationsstück) and its chief exponent Eduard von Bauernfeld (1802–1890). This popular playwright — who, incidentally, belonged to Schubert's circle of friends — was the most successful exponent of this type of social comedy: contemporary in setting, with largely conventional plots involving deftly drawn characters from the nobility and bourgeoisie, distinguished by its easy conversational style and fluency of dialogue. Bauernfeld's plays were a mainstay of the repertoire of Vienna's Burgtheater up to the early part of the twentieth century. The character study *Crises* (1852) has especially been singled out as one which served Hofmannsthal for creative stimulus and as a dramatic counterpart for his work on *An Impossible Man*. Even the opening stage directions, the palatial setting, the references to the card game and dance music drifting in from the adjoining ballroom, are close in spirit to the setting in Acts II and III of the later comedy. But Hofmannsthal has only drawn upon a number of externals from this popular genre: a precisely observed social framework and the manners and idiom appropriate to it; i.e. polished, polite social banter. What is lacking in Bauernfeld is any critical awareness of the conventional: there is no trace of parody in his language of the salon. The dimension of acute language-consciousness, that is, dialogue replete with critical irony, belongs to Hofmannsthal alone. Baron Hohenberg in *Crises* is, like Hans Karl Bühl (these names, meaning 'high mountain' and 'hillock' respectively, are linked by ironic allusion) are on the brink of forty, consequently at a 'critical' stage in life. There are also striking similarities in the confidential manners of the manservants in the two plays, and that semblance of desultoriness in the handling of dialogue which imperceptibly moves the action forward but conveys a static impression.

A less obvious, yet significant connection is to be traced to Granville-Barker's play *Waste* (1906/7), to which Hofmannsthal's attention was drawn by a review he read in *Die Schaubühne* in January 1908. This topical social drama, dealing with Disestablishment of the Church and rather loosely entitled a 'Tragedy', is concerned with the unfortunate consequences of a casual liaison between a member of parliament with brilliant career prospects and an unhappily married woman. Henry Trebell is described as: 'hard-bitten, brainy, forty-five and very sure of himself. He has a cold keen eye, which rather belies a sensitive mouth: hands which grip, and a figure that is austere.' These characteristics are, on the face of it, quite inapplicable to Hofmannsthal's comic hero, who is irresolute, *difficile* and lacking any firmness of hand. Common to both, however, is a problematical relationship to the opposite sex, indecision at crucial moments, inhibited self-expression, an incapacity for self-surrender, but a deep sense of the importance of the child. Trebell at times uses words which might have been uttered by Hans Karl: 'A prolonged fit of idleness might make me marry … a clever woman.' 'You know I never make promises … it's taking oneself too seriously.' 'There are three facts in life that call up emotion … Birth, Death, and the Desire for Children'. Unlike Hans Karl he is a self-confessed misogynist, but like him, he maintains excellent relations with an elder sister who lives with him under the same roof. Though Hofmannsthal develops his characters with varying degrees of irony, there is also a sufficient element of the ironical in Granville-Barker's subtle scripting of dialogue to stimulate the comic playwright. Absolute purity of genre, as between comedy and tragedy, is something modern social drama has dispensed with, at least since Anton Chehov's tragi-comedies conquered the stage. There is, indeed, a strong affinity between the virtually plotless, static Chehovian dramatic construct and that adopted by Hofmannsthal. There are equally many points of similarity between the lethargic, philandering Platonov and the passive heart-breaker Hans Karl. The point of focus is an individualized human portrait, not a comic type, even though Hofmannsthal's title (*Der Schwierige*) would seem to validate a universal condition. However, Hans Karl is hardly conceived in typological terms: the quality of being '*difficile*' is not a generic trait like avarice, hypocrisy, misanthropy or hypochondria. Hofmannsthal's play may allude by its title to the classical tradition of high comedy, but its treatment of the irreducible complexity of the individual psyche is specific and essentially modernist. One of his aphorisms in the collection *Buch der Freunde* (*Book of Friends*) pointedly states: 'The Individual is inexpressible'. In view of this, the choice of an indefinite article in the newly rendered title here adopted, appears to my mind justified. Everything points to Hans Karl being a singular case.

III

Hofmannsthal's struggle with the form of his most widely acclaimed comedy over rather more than a decade was anything but smooth progress. The precise date of its inception cannot exactly be pin-pointed, though the year 1907 has been widely acknowledged as marking the poet's resolute turn to prose comedy. There were three phases during which he worked on the text, whilst at the same time being engaged on other projects: (a) December 1909 to autumn 1911; (b) the latter half of 1917, when the greater part of the text took shape; (c) September 1919 to August 1920 when Act III was re-written and the manuscript prepared for publication. The play was first printed in successive issues of the journal *Neue Freie Presse* (Vienna, 1920). This was destined not to be the final version, however, for the tireless author undertook some further revisions for the publication in book form by Samuel Fischer (Berlin, 1921). The latter has become the standard text, now generally established as authoritative. Though many of the early draft manuscripts, including the first type-script, have been lost, a considerable body of material has survived and has been published in volume 12 of the collected critical edition, S. Fischer (Frankfurt a. M., 1993). To delve into this mass of trial formulations, variants, deletions and revisions, is to observe the perfectionist craftsman in his workshop, honing down his material, discarding what is felt to be inapt, superfluous, too bluntly expressed, wanting in finesse of tone or somehow out of character. Above all, Hofmannsthal was intent on strict economy of verbal means and on maintaining the appropriate tone. There are also numerous annotations designed to serve as signals or reminders as to mode and style, e.g.: 'One writes comedies not with wit but with sympathy.' 'Criticism as motor of the action.' 'Analogies: that someone barrs himself from his own happiness out of delicacy: Minna von Barnhelm. That all the figures consist of criticism: Misanthrope.' 'The conversation to be kept completely on the surface, Molière-like. Nothing of the subliminal emerges.' 'In Molière the essence lies not in the figures but in the relationships.' Such notes serve us as illuminating comments on the comedy as a whole and remind us of the fine tuning which has gone into its texture.

The prolonged genesis of this comedy reveals a changing focus in the conception of the central figures and their roles. Initially, Hofmannsthal had thought of calling the play 'Die Schwierigen' (The Difficult Couple) since not only Hans Karl but Helen too was to appear full of inhibiting complexities that stood in the way of any match between them. Another title considered by the author was 'Der Mann ohne Absicht' (The Man without Design) since this narrowed attention to that negative capability in the hero's constitution which might serve to illumine his dilemma. The shift of emphasis to a central figure of apparent inscrutabilty about whom all the other characters are grouped in speculative curiosity, gave the comedy greater strictness of design and focus without forfeiting the significance of the other protagonist, Helen. What Hofmannsthal was successful in achieving by this shift, was to accentuate the elements of confusion and misunderstanding, which became his principal motor in the mechanism of the comedy, not to mention their prominent motivic function. It is typical of Hofmannsthal's creative method that he should begin with a vivid idea of a character's personality and produce from this nucleus of essential human traits the appropriate speech, accents, atmospheric touches, which ultimately grew into the finished dialogue. Some of those who knew Hofmannsthal personally were quick to seize on the similarity between the author and the figure of Hans Karl. Paul Geraldy remarked: 'That is Hofmannsthal, shy, anxious, unable to act because he is too intelligent.' Such a view is, inevitably, over-simplified. A late annotation by Hofmannsthal (dated 5 November 1926) in retrospect affords truer insight as to his own detached view of his hero's representative status and significance: 'Attitude: social — Austrian (the "refined clever Viennese"). Connection to a tradition. Intended mediation. (Attitude of the "Difficult Man" in a world lacking nuance.)'

IV

The precise date at which the action of the comedy is set may be gleaned from a few scenes in the first Act (2, 3 and 8). It is ostensibly the twelfth of September 1917, about a year before the cessation of hostilities in World War I and at an historical juncture, since by then the Austro-Hungarian empire was rapidly falling apart. At that stage of the war the uneasy alliance between Prussia and Austria was further strained when Austro-Hungary undertook secret negotiations with the Entente powers to sue for peace. Hofmannsthal's schematic polemic entitled 'Prussian and Austrian' published in that critical year of 1917, is a revealing document not just in historical terms, but from the perspective of the comedy also. It crystallizes in controversial terms the deep-reaching social, cultural, historical and psychological differences which divided the brothers-in-arms. When fleshed out in terms of stage characters, we may recognize quite a number of these diametrically opposed or sharply contrasted traits in Neuhoff and Hans Karl. As with all abstract generalizations concerning national character and typologies, a reductive tendency to over-simplification and bias is inherent in the attempt. Consequently it is difficult to overlook the satirical brush with which Neuhoff the Prussian is tarred.

This comedy is concerned with the complications of human relations, not with the complexities of history. Allusions to the war regularly punctuate the text yet remain resolutely unobtrusive, being thrust into a background of more or less casual reference. It is not so much the recollection of a soldier dying of his wounds in hospital which receives accentuation, as the transparent contrivance by a Neuhoff to exploit the episode for his own conceited purposes. For in flattering Hans Karl and singing the praises of Helen's personality, he is clearly revelling in his own mental powers of perceptiveness and surmise as a reader of character. Equally, the incident of being buried alive in the trenches, related by Hans Karl to Helen, serves a higher revelatory function within their relationship rather than to introduce any authentic historical note. It is also apropos of Hans Karl's affair with Antoinette that some precise calendar dates are mentioned. These appear to anchor the play in an exact and purposeful time-scheme, yet actually serve a purely comic purpose when the over-scrupulous private secretary Neugebauer rattles them off from memory. The Emperor Franz Joseph I had been dead since 12 November 1916, and though the monarchy survived for the duration of the war, it was clearly as moribund as its personified symbol. The fact that Hans Karl should be pestered about a maiden speech to the Upper House in Parliament (which actually had ceased to be) is yet another of those anachronisms in the comedy which serve an ironic function. The entire social atmosphere, the insouciant demeanour of the characters pursuing their wonted pleasures and pastimes, all suggest that the war is a thing of the past while nothing in the fabric of society appears to have changed.

All of this accords with the author's purpose in representing society not analytically, but in suggestive or symbolic terms. In one of his aphorisms he posits this as a generally valid premise: 'Whoever sees the social whole other than symbolically goes astray.' A letter to his friend Arthur Schnitzler (2 November 1919) puts the case in more explicit terms:

> Perhaps I might never have been able to depict the society it [the comedy] represents, namely Austrian aristocratic society, with such love, in all its charm and distinction, than at that historical moment when all that had but recently been a given certainty, indeed a power, quietly and eerily dissolves into nothingness, just like a little lingering cloud of morning mist.

The playwright's approach is not designed to achieve social-historical authenticity, however finely attuned he might be to the symptoms and nuances of his transient epoch. His preferred method is to capture the spirit of the times through the various facets of character and language. A revealing passage from a letter to his friend Raoul Auernheimer (20 August 1921) sounds out an important distinction in their respective understanding of the role of the central figure in the play as representative of something more complex:

> We do indeed look for the groundwork on which the character of a 'Difficult Man'
> rests in quite different spheres: you, within the social, which seems to me of
> secondary importance, I, within one that is deeper: in the difficult relationship to
> speech and action, those twin magical forces which form links between human
> beings. Herein also lies the justification for that comico-antithetical relationship
> fundamental to this comedy, and to his counterpart Stani to whom speech and
> action come so easily.

Faced with a play that contains so many layers of possible meaning, closer scrutiny
of Hofmannsthal's central figure and his relationship to language would seem to be
called for.

V

The so-called 'language crisis' that beset the young Hofmannsthal, exactly coincided
with the turn of the century and found expression in his famous 'Chandos Letter' ('Ein
Brief', 1902), as it came to be called. This fictive letter is addressed to the creator of
the essay, Sir Francis Bacon, by a young contemporary who finds himself in an acute
dilemma: though a practised, accomplished writer, Chandos has lost faith in the
efficacy of words, since for him the very medium of language has become meaningless
and stale. He analyzes his condition with profound introspection, paradoxically
employing the most eloquent terms in offering a diagnosis of his paralyzing condition:

> My case is, briefly, this: I have totally lost the capacity either to think or to speak
> coherently about anything whatsoever.
>   At first it gradually became impossible for me to discuss a more demanding or
> general topic and thereby to have recourse to such words as are commonly and
> casually employed by everyone. I felt an inexplicable malaise in merely uttering
> the words 'mind', 'soul' or 'body'. I found it inwardly impossible to pronounce
> any judgement on the affairs at court, the events at parliament or whatever. And
> this was not because of any form of scruples, for you know my all but frivolous
> courage and frankness: but rather those abstract words which our tongue must of
> necessity employ to voice any sort of judgement, fell apart in my mouth like putrid
> mushrooms.

This essay by Hofmannsthal touched a nerve among his contemporaries and he was
quickly recognized as the spokesman of a generation of writers who felt a radical
break with the literature of the past. The problematical nature of language never
ceased to be an issue for Hofmannsthal or the writers of Young Vienna. He noted on
5 October 1909: 'Speech is a tremendous compromise for everybody — only this
seldom becomes conscious, because it constitutes the universal means of making
oneself understood.' This observation leads one straight to an important theme of the
comedy. Language, as the chief medium of communication and the indispensable
vehicle of social intercourse, itself becomes the focus of attention in *An Impossible
Man*. Hans Karl's exasperated words in the penultimate scene may be recalled here:
'But everything one utters is indecent. The simple fact that one utters something is

indecent.' His suspicion of the word is one of his principal characteristics and is chiefly expressed through his frequent lapses into silence, his inability to commit himself, his recourse to evasive gesture and, most tellingly, his delight in Furlani's delicate act of mimicry. The dumbshow by this entertainer (whose act is merely described in Act II) is to be seen as a meaningful correlative to the social role played by his admirer Hans Karl, who finds in Furlani 'more intellect than for most conversations'. Helen too is severely censorious of all conversation in so-called polite society: 'words which reduce to banality everything that is real and make a sedative out of small-talk.' It is a significant feature of this sophisticated text that key terms resonate in motivic manner and thereby produce a subtle network of associations. Most prominent among such words are: 'Absicht' (intention, design), 'Nuance', 'Mißverständnis' (misunderstanding), 'Konfusion', 'Komplikation', 'Notwendigkeit' (necessity). The translator of this comedy is therefore challenged throughout to maintain consistency within a variety of contexts which subtly ring changes on stress and meaning.

A key to Hofmannsthal's sensitive treatment of the theme of human communication may be found *in nuce* by looking at an early poem entitled 'Die Beiden'. The poem was obviously recalled to mind when he wrote the final scene in Act II, since the stage direction referring to the lovers' hands which fail to meet is virtual self-quotation. The poem's symbolic encounter involves only dumb gesture, movement, and the all-expressive human hand to convey notions of self-control, deep, unsettling emotion, and the failure to communicate something precious, symbolized in the cup filled with wine. Not a word is spoken, yet the subtle, complex import of a momentous encounter between the sexes is nonetheless vividly made present. Such is the quality of Hofmannsthal's reticent art, that sign and symbol evoke a profuser intensity of meaning than any denotative terms or direct speech. The dialogue which Hofmannsthal developed for his comedy frequently gives way to the suggestive force of gesture and silence. The discreet manservant Luke can read his master's mind and mood by observing tell-tale signs of his agitation, like the unnecessary opening of a drawer or the straightening of a picture. At a higher level of sophistication, Helen has learnt to read Hans Karl's hidden biography by closely observing his inconsequential affairs with a succession of women. The comic corollary of such insight is Stani's misplaced conviction that he can understand every nuance of his uncle, or Neuhoff's haughty verdict on Hans Karl as a 'nonentity', and not least, the generally wrong-headed interpretation of his 'intentions' by most of the characters who surround him. As a figure, Hans Karl stands at the centre of endless, futile speculation. He is besieged by characters who look for hidden meanings in his conduct where none exists. The irony of this situation is exploited to the full in a comedy which has for its focus an eligible bachelor who cannot make up his mind about anything, least of all about women. Language figures in all of this as the flawed medium of communication, brimming with ambiguities, misused and misinterpreted by all, yet for all its fallibility, still the indispensable vehicle of social interaction. Hans Karl and Helen, in two crucial scenes together that are vital to their mutual understanding (Act II, Sc. 14 and

Act III, Sc. 8), come to reveal their true selves just because there is no trace of make-believe in their 'authentic' use of language, so different from the smooth dissimulations of a Neuhoff or the pompous verbosity of the Famous Man.

Each character in the comedy is defined by distinctive verbal registers and individual mannerisms of speech, which includes even the minor figures. The servants Luke and Vincent are sharply contrasted by their respective manner and tone; the former is dignified and discreet in an old-fashioned way, the latter an uncouth, rough-spoken representative of the brash new age that is about to break in. Neugebauer uses the obsequious, over-solicitous terms of a resentful and avid, upwardly mobile petit-bourgeoisie: a voice rather reminiscent of a Uriah Heep. The Famous Man is academic vanity personified, expressing himself with bloated pretentiousness. Edine, foremost of the blue-stockings, is all foolish frills, with comic lapses into malapropism and the vulgar vernacular. Agatha is a scaled-down image of her mistress Antoinette, and even less successful in preventing her voluble tongue from uttering indiscretions. Hechingen's usual tone is anxious, fussy and tedious, but when he alters it towards his wife to heightened ardour and flamboyance, the unwonted romantic note becomes irritating to her. Neuhoff, the Prussian, uses speech most artificially, either as a flattering tool to ingratiate himself, or as a wooer's weapon to beguile and conquer, or as the badge of intellectual superiority in a society he secretly despises. The flighty Antoinette is perfectly captured in the nervous, coquettish idiom of her feminine role, displaying the native charm of Viennese at its most appealing. Crescence and Altenwyl belong to the well-groomed nobility and do it full justice by their easy eloquence, enlivened by that subtle admixture of colloquial Viennese which binds the upper with the lower social orders and which translation can only hint at. Stani's speech with its clipped conciseness and somewhat juvenile self-certainty betrays his weakness for over-hasty simplification, snap judgements and ineptitude as the fond imitator of his uncle Kari. By this finely tuned polyphonous treatment of the voices of the play, Hofmannsthal unfolds the full register of implicit ironies with great virtuosity.

In that concisest of aphorisms, already quoted, Hofmannsthal draws attention to the incommensurable nature of human personality: 'The individual is inexpressible.' Language must, in such a view, fall short of expressing the entire truth about anyone; yet this comedy is expressly designed to delve into so complex a character as Hans Karl. Hofmannsthal's hero is both egotistical and enigmatic; one who rather relishes the fact that nobody, not even his closest relatives, can sound out his whims and fancies, much less fathom his deeper designs (in so far as he harbours any). He applies the indeterminate adjective 'impossible' to himself on three occasions within two lengthy dialogues with Helen. Whether prompted by sheer frustration ('My God, I'm just impossible'), by insecurity or more artful self-reproach, the word resonates with shifting accentuation and meaning. If it is also used in sweeping condemnation of Neuhoff and Vinzenz this reveals its multi-faceted function within the finely-woven texture of Hofmannsthal's language. Significantly Helen says of him: 'it's impossible to know his final word on anything'. He once says to Helen in his own defence: 'I have an impossible character', yet to Crescence he protests: 'I'm the least complicated person in the world.' There is a considerable portion of truth in both assertions. Helen, with her profound feminine intuition, is able to see into the heart of the man she has always loved. She commands more searching means of understanding Hans Karl than mere words can provide, for she judges him by his actions and demeanour, as when he involuntarily returns to her house having said goodbye, or by meanings that lie beyond the reach of words as attested by the no less involuntary proposal scene (Act III, Sc. 8). He has every right to be amazed at her ability to interpret his every word and action. She has had access to that deeper will within the unconscious self which Hans Karl is afraid to address, until she breaks the spell by her insistent probing. What sublime irony ultimately lies in this effortless apprehension of an impossibly difficult man.

* * *

Note: The first stage performance of *Der Schwierige* took place, without the author being present, on 8 November 1921 in the 'Residenztheater' Munich, directed by Kurt Stieler. The first staging in Vienna was on 6 April 1924 in the 'Theater in der Josephstadt', directed by Max Reinhardt. This was attended by Hugo von Hofmannsthal.

An Impossible Man

Comedy in Three Acts

by
Hugo von Hofmannsthal

DRAMATIS PERSONAE

HANS KARL BÜHL

CRESCENCE, his Sister

STANI, her Son

HELEN ALTENWYL

ALTENWYL

ANTOINETTE HECHINGEN

HECHINGEN

NEUHOFF

EDINE

NANNI } Antoinette's Friends

HUBERTA

AGATHA, Lady's Maid

NEUGEBAUER, Confidential Secretary

LUKE, Principal Manservant in Hans Karl's Household

VINCENT, a new Servant

A FAMOUS MAN

Servants in the Bühl and Altenwyl Households

FIRST ACT

Medium-sized room in one of Vienna's historical town-houses, appointed as the master of the house's study.

SCENE ONE

Enter LUKE *with* VINCENT.

LUKE
This is the so-called study. Only relatives and close friends are shown in here; or else, if expressly stated, into the green room.

VINCENT *steps forward*
What's his line of work? Estate management? Or what? Something in politics?

LUKE
His secretary comes in through this folding door.

VINCENT
He's got a private secretary too? They're just the dregs, they are! Career failures! Does he have any clout with him?

LUKE
This way leads to the dressing room. We'll go in there now and lay out evening dress and tails, for him to choose as he pleases: that's because nothing specific has been ordered.

VINCENT *noses about all the furniture*
Well what then? You wanted to show me the ropes. That could wait till tomorrow morning, and meanwhile we might have a friendly little chat as colleagues. I'm fully aware of what serving a gentleman means, and have been for years. So just stick to the essentials: by that I mean all the nitty-gritty. So what then? Let's hear it.

LUKE *straightens a picture that is not hanging quite straight*
He can't abide seeing a picture or a mirror hanging crooked. When he starts opening all the drawers and looking for a mislaid key, then he's really in a bad mood.

VINCENT
Cut out all the silly little details. Now you just told me that his sister and his nephew, who live in the house with him, are also to be announced every time.

LUKE *busily dusts a mirror with his handkerchief*
The same as with any visitors. He's very strict about that.

VINCENT

What's behind all this? No doubt he wants to keep them at arm's length. Why does he let them live here then? He must have several houses? They're his heirs, aren't they? Surely they must wish him dead.

LUKE

Our Countess Crescence and Count Stani? God forbid! I can't think what to make of you.

VINCENT

Never mind your opinions. What purpose can he have then, keeping them in the house? That's what interests me. Why? Because it throws light on certain intentions. I've got to know about these before I sign up with him.

LUKE

On what kind of 'certain intentions'?

VINCENT

Don't repeat my words! This is a very serious business for me. All being well, this could mean lodgings for the rest of my life. Once you've retired as manager of his affairs, I'll take matters in hand good and proper. This house might just suit me, by all I hear. But I want to know just where I stand. If he settles these relatives in his home, it pretty well means that he's about to start a new life. At his age, and after the war's over, that makes pretty good sense. Once you've got forty years on your back. —

LUKE

His Lordship's fortieth birthday is next year.

VINCENT

In a nutshell, he wants to cut down on his flings with women. He's had enough of these shenanigans.

LUKE

I don't understand your blather.

VINCENT

But of course you understand me only too well, Squire. — All this tallies quite neatly with what the porter's wife told me. Everything now boils down to this. Does he have any plans on getting married? In that case a legitimate female regime will take over the house, and where does that leave me? — Or else he wants to share his last years as bachelor with me! So let's have all your thoughts on the subject. That's the point and the true nub of the matter for me.

LUKE *clears his throat.*

VINCENT

Why are you trying to scare me?

LUKE
He sometimes stands there in the room without you hearing his footsteps.

VINCENT
What's his game? Does he want to catch people out? Is he actually that crafty?

LUKE
In that case you simply have to disappear in silence.

VINCENT
These are disgusting habits of his. I'll soon cure him of those and no mistake.

SCENE TWO

HANS KARL *who has come in quietly*
You can stay, Luke. Is that you, Neugebauer?

VINCENT *stands to the side in the dark.*

LUKE
Beg to report, your Lordship, that's the new manservant who was with his Highness Prince Palm for four years.

HANS KARL
Carry on as you were with him. Ask Mr. Neugebauer to come over with the files concerning Hohenbühl. Otherwise I'm at home to no one. *A bell is heard.*

LUKE
That's the bell in the small vestibule. *Leaves.*

VINCENT *remains.*

HANS KARL *has stepped over to the writing desk.*

SCENE THREE

LUKE *enters and announces*
The Countess Freudenberg.

CRESCENCE *has come in immediately behind him.*

LUKE *withdraws,* VINCENT *likewise.*

CRESCENCE
Am I disturbing you, Kari? Pardon me —

HANS KARL
But my dear Crescence.

CRESCENCE
I was just going upstairs to dress — for the soiree.

HANS KARL
At Altenwyl's place?

CRESCENCE
Surely you'll also be putting in an appearance? Or not? I only wish to know, dear.

HANS KARL
If it's all the same to you, I might possibly make up my mind a bit later, and possibly ring up from the Mess. You know, I do so object to being tied down.

CRESCENCE
Oh, indeed.

HANS KARL
But if you were counting on me —

CRESCENCE
My dear Kari, I'm quite old enough to drive home alone — and anyhow, Stani is coming to fetch me. So you're not coming?

HANS KARL
I should like to think about it.

CRESCENCE
A soiree does not become more attractive by thinking about it, my dear. And then I had the impression that out there you'd rather lost the habit of thinking too much about things. *Sits down beside him as he stands at the desk.* Be an angel, Kari, and don't persist in that touchiness, that abruptness, indecisiveness, which could erupt in such fierce feuds with your friends; and only because one calls you a hypochondriac, another a spoilsport, a third, someone who can't be relied upon. — You returned home in such an excellent frame of mind; you're quite the same as you were at twenty-two, when I was almost in love with my brother.

HANS KARL
My dear good Crescence, are you paying me compliments?

CRESCENCE
But of course not; I'm putting things as they are: in such matters, Stani is an infallible judge. He finds you quite simply the leading gentlemen of the upper classes. He speaks of his Uncle Kari at every turn; one can't pay him a greater compliment than to say that he looks like you, and he does, you know — in his movements he's quite your second self — he knows of nothing more elegant than the way you treat people — the grand manner, the sense of distance you convey to everyone — and the complete even-handedness and bonhomie towards even the humblest — but he has, of course, tumbled to your weaknesses, just as I have; he

worships decisiveness, strength, all that's definite; he hates shilly-shallying, in that he's just like me!

CRESCENCE

HANS KARL

I congratulate you on your son, Crescence. I feel sure that you will always take great pleasure in him.

CRESCENCE

But — to get back to matters in hand; good heavens, if one has gone through what you went through, and then behaved as if it were nothing —

HANS KARL *embarrassed*

But everyone has done that!

CRESCENCE

Now, pardon me, by no means everyone! But then I'd have thought that one might have mastered one's neurotic foibles.

HANS KARL

I still have these when faced with people in a drawing room. A soiree is a nightmare for me; I simply can't help myself there. I can just about grasp that there are people who like to entertain, but not that there are people who want to go to these things.

CRESCENCE

What are you afraid of then? One must surely be able to discuss the matter. Do the older folk bore you?

HANS KARL

Oh, but they're quite charming, they're so well-behaved.

CRESCENCE

Or do the young get on your nerves?

HANS KARL

I have nothing against them. It's the thing itself that is such a nuisance, you know; everything — the whole business is such a frightful tangle of misunderstandings. Oh, these everlasting misunderstandings!

CRESCENCE

After all that you've had to go through out there at the front, I find it incomprehensible that you haven't developed a thicker skin.

HANS KARL

Crescence, that doesn't make one any less sensitive, but rather more so. How is it you don't understand this? I find the tears starting over some silly nonsense — or I get quite hot with shame over the merest trifle, over a nuance which nobody notices; or again, it might happen that I say out aloud what I'm thinking — under these circumstances, it's quite impossible to go mixing with people. I simply can't define it further, but it's more than I can take. To be honest, I gave notice two hours ago that I was calling off the Altenwyls. Perhaps another soiree some time soon, but not this one.

CRESCENCE
Not this one. So why not this one exactly?

HANS KARL
It's just more than I can take, purely in general terms.

CRESCENCE
When you say 'in general terms' you mean something specific.

HANS KARL
Not in the slightest, Crescence.

CRESCENCE
But of course. Aha, well I can set your mind at rest on that score.

HANS KARL
On what score?

CRESCENCE
As regards Helen.

HANS KARL
What makes you mention Helen?

CRESCENCE
My dear, I'm neither deaf nor blind; moreover, Helen has from the fifteenth year of her life until quite recently, well, let's say up to the second year of the war, been head over heels in love with you. For this I have concrete evidence on a whole number of counts.

HANS KARL
Now listen, Crescence, you're simply imagining things —

CRESCENCE
Do you know that in the past, some three or four years ago, when she was quite a young debutante, I had the notion that she might be the one person in the world who could pin you down, who could become your wife. But now I'm utterly delighted it didn't come to this. Two such complicated people; that spells trouble.

HANS KARL
You do me too much honour. I'm the least complicated person in the world. *He has pulled out a drawer in his desk.* But I can't think how you got the idea — I'm attached to Helen, she's a sort of cousin, after all; I've known her since she was so little — she could be my daughter.

CRESCENCE
Mine more likely. But I don't want her for a daughter. And I certainly don't want that Baron Neuhoff for a son-in-law.

HANS KARL
Neuhoff? Is it that serious a business?

CRESCENCE
She is going to marry him.

HANS KARL *slams the drawer shut.*

CRESCENCE
I see it as a *fait accompli*, despite the fact that he is an outlandish fellow blown in from some East Prussian province or other at the back of beyond …

HANS KARL
Geography never was your forte, Crescence; the Neuhoffs are a Holstein family.

CRESCENCE
That's all much of a muchness. In short, outlandish people.

HANS KARL
As it happens, a family of the first rank. As well connected as it is possible to be.

CRESCENCE
Now I ask you, it's listed in the Almanach de Gotha after all. And then, who can check up on it from where we stand?

HANS KARL
You are rather fired up against the fellow, aren't you?

CRESCENCE
Well it's enough to get one's goat! If one of the finest girls, such as Helen, gets a bee in her bonnet over some outlandish fellow, despite the fact that he'll never in a lifetime rank anywhere with us —

HANS KARL
You think so?

CRESCENCE
Not in a lifetime, despite the fact that she's quite immune to his suavity; in a word, despite herself and our world —

A brief pause.

HANS KARL *pulls out another drawer with some vehemence.*

CRESCENCE
May I help you to look? You're making me nervous.

HANS KARL
Thanks awfully, no. I'm not actually looking for anything. I was trying the wrong key.

SECRETARY *appears in the small doorway*
Oh, I do most humbly beg your pardon.

HANS KARL
I'll be free any moment now, my dear Neugebauer.

SECRETARY *withdraws.*

CRESCENCE *steps up to the table*
Kari, if I could only do you one little favour, I'd scotch this entire affair.

HANS KARL
What sort of affair?

CRESCENCE
The one we were speaking of: Helen and Neuhoff. I'd scotch it in two shakes.

HANS KARL
What?

CRESCENCE
I could swear to it that she's just as much in love with you today as six years ago, and that it requires only a word, the merest shadow of a hint —

HANS KARL
Which I beseech you by all that's holy not to mention —

CRESCENCE
Oh well, all right then. That too, I promise.

HANS KARL
My dear sister, with all due respect for your energetic ways, but people are not, thank goodness, quite that simple.

CRESCENCE
My dear brother, people are, thank goodness, quite simple if one takes them simply. I can see then that this piece of news is not a great blow to you. All the better — you've lost interest in Helen, I am now duly informed.

HANS KARL *rising*
But I don't know how you arrived at the idea that I should even find it necessary to lose interest. And do other people entertain these bizarre notions too?

CRESCENCE
Very probably.

HANS KARL
Do you know, this actually whets my appetite to go there?

CRESCENCE
So as to give Theophil your blessing? He will indeed be charmed. He'll completely debase himself just to gain intimate acquaintance with you.

HANS KARL
Don't you think it would have been right and proper, under the circumstances, for me to have shown my face at the Altenwyls' long ago? I'm terribly sorry now that I said I couldn't come.

CRESCENCE
Then let them be rung back again: it was all a misunderstanding through a new servant and that you will be coming.

LUKE *enters.*

HANS KARL *to* CRESCENCE
You know, I should still like to think about it.

LUKE
I respectfully beg leave to announce someone presently.

CRESCENCE *to* LUKE
I'm going. Ring Count Altenwyl quickly to say that his Lordship will be attending this evening. There's been a misunderstanding.

LUKE *looks at* HANS KARL.

HANS KARL *without looking at* LUKE
You would then have to ring up the Mess first, of course, saying that I must ask Count Hechingen not to wait for me for dinner, and not afterwards either.

CRESCENCE
Of course. He'll do that at once. But first ring Count Altenwyl, so that these good people know where they stand.

Exit LUKE.

CRESCENCE *stands up*
There, and now I shall leave you to your affairs. *While walking off* With which Hechingen did you have the engagement? With Nandi?

HANS KARL
No, With Adolf.

CRESCENCE *comes back*
With Antoinette's husband? Isn't he a complete ninny?

HANS KARL
You know, Crescence, I simply can't be the judge of that. I find, as time goes by, that in conversation all so-called cleverness is stupid, and the stupid tends rather to sound clever —

CRESCENCE
And I remain convinced that there's more to him than there is to her.

HANS KARL
You know, I never really knew him in the past, or *he has turned towards the wall and adjusts a picture that hangs crooked* only as the husband of his wife — and then out there, we formed a friendship. You know, he is such a thoroughly decent fellow. We were together in the winter of 1915, holding a position for twenty weeks in the Carpathian forests, I with my riflemen and he with his pioneers; and we shared our very last piece of bread with one another. I developed great respect for him. There were a good many decent chaps out there, but I never saw one who in face of death maintained such calm, almost a sort of comfortable ease.

CRESCENCE
If his relatives could hear you speak, they would hug you. So go to this fool of a woman and reconcile her with the fellow: you'll make two families happy. This vague notion of divorce or separation (it's all much of a muchness) eternally hanging over them, is getting on everyone's nerves. And anyhow, it would only benefit you if the whole affair were to be knocked into some sort of shape.

HANS KARL
How do you mean?

CRESCENCE
Well now, to tell you straight: there are those who vent the idiotic notion that if the marriage could be annulled, you would marry her.

HANS KARL *is silent.*

CRESCENCE
I don't say they are serious-minded people who spread this far-fetched nonsense about.

HANS KARL *is silent.*

CRESCENCE
Have you paid her a visit since you came back from the front?

HANS KARL
No, I should of course.

CRESCENCE *looking to one side*
Then visit her tomorrow and have a good heart to heart talk.

HANS KARL *bends down as if to pick something up*
I really don't know if I'm the right person for the job.

CRESCENCE
You'd actually be performing a good deed. By this you will clearly give her to understand that she was up the garden path a couple of years ago, when she was doing her utmost to parade herself with you.

HANS KARL *without looking at her*
That's just a whim of yours.

CRESCENCE
Precisely the way she has today set her sights on Stani.

HANS KARL *astonished*
Your son Stani?

CRESCENCE
Ever since the Spring. *She had reached the door, but turns back once more and comes over to the desk.* You could do me a great favour there, Kari.

HANS KARL
But I beg you, for heaven's sake, do say! *He offers her a seat, she remains standing.*

CRESCENCE
I'll send Stani down to you for a moment. Make the position clear to him. Tell him that Antoinette — is a woman who compromises one for no good reason. In short, put him off her.

HANS KARL
Now, how do you imagine this to be done? If he's in love with her?

CRESCENCE
But men aren't ever that much in love, and you are the oracle for Stani, aren't you? If you could use mere conversation for the purpose — promise?

HANS KARL
Well, you know — if an easy transition can be found —

CRESCENCE *has walked over to the door again, speaks from there*
You'll manage to find the right way. You have no idea what authority you possess in his eyes.

About to leave, she turns round again, walks right up to the desk. Tell him you find her lacking in finesse — and that you were never involved with her. That will make him drop her on the spot. *She goes over to the door again, the same performance.* You know, don't say it too sharply to him, but not all that lightly either. Not too much of 'between ourselves'. And see to it that he doesn't in the least suspect that it comes from me — he's got the fixed idea that I want to marry him off. Of course I do, but

— he's not to know it: in that he's so like you: the merest hint that one is trying to influence him — ! *Once more the same performance.* You know, I'm most anxious that this is said today; why lose a whole evening? In that way you'll also have your planned programme: you must make it clear to Antoinette how much you disapprove of the whole thing — you must put her in mind of her marriage — you can sing Adolf's praises — and so you have a mission, and the entire evening will have some point for you.

She goes out.

SCENE FOUR

VINCENT *has entered from the right. He first looks about to see if* CRESCENCE *has left, then:*
I don't know if the head servant has announced that there's a youngish person waiting outside, a lady's maid or the like —

HANS KARL
What's it all about?

VINCENT
She has come from the Countess Hechingen, actually. She seems sort of private and confidential. *Stepping even closer.* She's not the poor and bashful sort.

HANS KARL
I'll see to all this myself. Show her in.

VINCENT *exit right.*

SCENE FIVE

LUKE *enters briskly through centre door*
May I respectfully enquire if anyone has been announced to your Lordship? Regarding the Countess Hechingen's own lady's maid, Agatha? I said I had no idea whether his Lordship was at home.

HANS KARL
Good. I've let it be known that I am. Have you telephoned Count Altenwyl?

LUKE
I humbly beg your Lordship's pardon. I noticed your Lordship did not wish to telephone, but also did not wish to contradict her Ladyship the Countess — so, for the time being, I have not telephoned.

HANS KARL *smiling*
Good, Luke.

LUKE *moves as far as the door.*

HANS KARL
Luke, how do you find the new servant?

LUKE *hesitantly*
One might possibly see how he fares.

HANS KARL
Impossible fellow. Pay him off. Send him packing!

LUKE
Very well, your Lordship. Just as I thought.

HANS KARL
Mention nothing this evening.

SCENE SIX

VINCENT *shows in* AGATHA. *Exeunt.*

HANS KARL
Good evening, Agatha.

AGATHA
Oh, your Grace, that I should be seeing your Lordship! I'm quite atremble.

HANS KARL
Won't you take a seat?

AGATHA
Oh, your Grace, please don't take it amiss that I've come in place of Mr.Brandstätter.

HANS KARL
But my dear Agatha, we are old acquaintances, aren't we? What brings you to me then?

AGATHA
Dear God, but your Lordship knows only too well. I've come because of the letters.

HANS KARL *is dismayed.*

AGATHA
Oh, pardon me, oh Lord, it's beyond belief how my Ladyship drilled it into me not to ruin things by my behaviour.

HANS KARL *hesitantly*
The Countess did indeed write to me saying that certain letters in my possession, which belong to her, would be collected by a certain Mr. Brandstätter on the

fifteenth. It's the twelfth today, but I can, of course, also hand the letters over to you. And on the spot, if the Countess so desires. I know only too well how devoted you are to the Countess.

AGATHA
Certain letters — how you say this, your Lordship. I am only too aware what letters they are.

HANS KARL *coolly*
I shall give orders at once.

AGATHA
If she could only see us together like this, my Ladyship. That would be some reassurance, a slight consolation.

HANS KARL *starts rummaging in a drawer.*

AGATHA
After these ghastly seven weeks, ever since we knew that our dear Count had returned from the front and we had no sign of life from him —

HANS KARL *looks up*
You've had no sign of life from Count Hechingen?

AGATHA
From him! When I say "our dear Count", in our language this means you, your Lordship! We don't refer to Count Hechingen as "our dear Count"!

HANS KARL *highly embarrassed*
Ah, pardon me, I wasn't to know that.

AGATHA *shyly*
Until this afternoon, we did still think there'd be a reunion at Count Altenwyl's soiree. Then the Countess Altenwyl's lady companion rang me to say: he has cried off!

HANS KARL *stands up.*

AGATHA
He's cried off, Agatha, my lady cried, cried off because he heard that I was coming! Then everything is over, and she fixes me with a glance that would melt a heart of stone.

HANS KARL *very politely, but with the wish to conclude matters*
I fear that I haven't got the letters in question here in my desk. I'll call my secretary at once.

AGATHA
Oh Lord, these letters are in the hands of a secretary! My Ladyship mustn't ever hear of this!

HANS KARL
The letters are sealed, naturally!

AGATHA
Sealed! So things have come to that!

HANS KARL *speaks into the telephone*
My dear Neugebauer, if you could just come over for a second! Yes, I'm free now — but without the files — it concerns something else. Straight away? No, do finish the calculations. In three minutes will do.

AGATHA
He musn't see me; he knows me from old times!

HANS KARL
You can step into the library. I'll put the light on for you.

AGATHA
How were we to imagine that everything would suddenly be over.

HANS KARL *on the point of conducting her across, stops, and frowns*
Dear Agatha, since you are in fact privy to everything, — I don't quite understand; I did write the Countess a long letter from the field hospital in the Spring.

AGATHA
Yes, that abominable letter.

HANS KARL
I don't understand. It was a most amicable letter.

AGATHA
It was a most deceitful letter. We were simply trembling as we read it, that letter. Made quite bitter we were, and humiliated!

HANS KARL
But for what reason, I do beseech you!

AGATHA *looks at him*
For the reason that you painted Count Hechingen in such glowing colours — and stated that when all's said and done, one man is as good as the next and anyone can be chosen to stand in for anyone else.

HANS KARL
But I didn't express myself like that at all. Those were simply never my thoughts!

AGATHA

At any rate, that was their meaning. Oh we read that letter over and over again! So this, cried my lady, this is the result of all those starry nights and lovelorn thoughts, this letter, where he tells me in dry-as-dust terms: one man is as good as the next, our love was just a fantasy, forget me, take Hechingen back again —

HANS KARL

But not a single word of this was in that letter.

AGATHA

It's not a question of words. We could gather the meaning all too clearly. That humiliating meaning, those degrading inferences. Oh, we know only too well. That trick of self-abasement is pure craftiness. When a man blames himself in a love affair, he is in fact blaming the affair. And in no time at all, we're the ones who end up being blamed.

HANS KARL *is silent.*

AGATHA *taking a step closer*

I really fought on behalf of our dear Count, as my Ladyship said: Agatha, you'll see, he wants to marry Countess Altenwyl and that's the only reason he wants to patch up my marriage.

HANS KARL

That was what the Countess suspected me of doing!

AGATHA

Those were her darkest hours, when she started brooding on this. Then a gleam of hope would appear. No, she would then cry out, her I need not fear, since she is running after him; and if a woman runs after Kari, she hasn't got a chance with him; she doesn't deserve him anyhow, since she hasn't got a heart.

HANS KARL *sets something or other straight*

If only I could convince you —

AGATHA

But then again her sudden fear —

HANS KARL

How remote from the truth all this is!

AGATHA

If he should get engaged to her before my very eyes —

HANS KARL

But how can the Countess —

AGATHA

Oh men do such things; but you won't, will you, your Lordship?

HANS KARL
Nothing in the world could be further from my thoughts, my dear Agatha.

AGATHA
Oh, I kiss your Lordship's hand! *Quickly kisses his hand.*

HANS KARL *withdraws his hand from her*
I hear my secretary coming.

AGATHA
Because we women know, naturally, that something so beautiful is not for all eternity. But that it should all suddendly end just for that, is something we can't quite accept!

HANS KARL
You will be seeing me then. I will let you have the letters personally and — Come in! Do come in, Neugebauer.

AGATHA *exit right.*

SCENE SEVEN

NEUGEBAUER *steps in*
Your Lordship called for me.

HANS KARL
If you'd have the kindness to help my memory a little. I'm looking for a bundle of letters — they're private letters, sealed — about two fingers thick.

NEUGEBAUER
With a date on them written by your Lordship? June 15th to 22nd of October 1916?

HANS KARL
Quite right. You know —

NEUGEBAUER
I had this file under my very hands, but can't for the moment quite recall. In the press and throng of activities amongst such a diversity of papers, which increase by the day —

HANS KARL *without a hint of reproach*
It baffles me how these purely private papers could have got among the files —

NEUGEBAUER
Were I to suspect that your Lordship casts the slightest shadow of a doubt on my discretion —

HANS KARL
But it never entered my mind.

NEUGEBAUER
May I be permitted to start looking at once; I shall exert all my powers to clarify this most regrettable occurrence.

HANS KARL
My dear Neugebauer, you attach far too much importance to the entire incident.

NEUGEBAUER
I have for some time remarked that something about me irritates your Lordship of late. True, the course of my education was directed solely towards the inner self, and if therefore I did not acquire flawless drawing-room manners, then this lack may perhaps be compensated in the eyes of a benevolent judge, by qualities which it would not readily lie in my character to have to underline myself.

HANS KARL
I don't doubt it for a moment, my dear Neugebauer. You give me the impression of being over-burdened. I must ask you to leave off a little earlier in the evening. Why not go for a walk every evening with your fiancée?

NEUGEBAUER *is silent.*

HANS KARL
If it is private worries which trouble you, perhaps I could be of service in some way by helping to ease the situation.

NEUGEBAUER
Your Lordship assumes that for our kind it could only be a matter of material concern.

HANS KARL
I didn't wish to say anything of that kind. I know that you are engaged to be married, and assuredly happy —

NEUGEBAUER
I'm not sure if your Lordship is alluding to the caretaker at Hohenbühl Castle?

HANS KARL
Yes indeed, the lady to whom you have been engaged these five years.

NEUGEBAUER
My present fiancee is the daughter of a civil servant of some standing. She was bride-to-be of my best friend who fell half a year ago. Even while her betrothed was alive, I was close in her affections — and I considered it a sacred legacy to the fallen friend to offer this young girl comfort and support for life.

HANS KARL *hesitantly*
And what of the former relationship of many years' standing?

NEUGEBAUER
That I dissolved, naturally. It goes without saying, in the noblest and most considerate manner possible.

HANS KARL
Ah!

NEUGEBAUER
Naturally I shall fulfil all due obligations entered upon in that direction, and will have to carry these over into the new partnership. No small matter, admittedly.

HANS KARL *is silent.*

NEUGEBAUER
Your Lordship may possibly not be able to gauge the harsh moral earnestness to which the lack-lustre lives of our social sphere is subject, or that it can for us only be a question of exchanging heavy duties for heavier ones still.

HANS KARL
I just thought that if one is getting married, one must look forward to it.

NEUGEBAUER
In our modest sphere the personal point of view cannot be the deciding factor.

HANS KARL
Of course it can't. Then you will try to find the letters for me if you can.

NEUGEBAUER
I shall search diligently, even if it takes until midnight. *Exit.*

HANS KARL *to himself*
What is it about me, that everybody is tempted to teach me some lesson or other, and that I'm never quite sure if they haven't the right to do so.

SCENE EIGHT

STANI *stands in the centre doorway in tails.*
Pardon me, just wanted to say 'good evening' to you, Uncle Kari, if one isn't intruding.

HANS KARL *had moved over to the right, but remains standing*
Not in the least. *Offers him a seat and a cigarette.*

STANI *takes the cigarette*
But of course it irks you if one comes in unannounced. In that you're just like me. I also hate it if anyone barges in on one. I always want to organize my thoughts a little first.

HANS KARL
Pray don't feel constrained, you're at home here, after all.

STANI
Ah forgive me, in your house I'm —

HANS KARL
Do sit down.

STANI
No really, I wouldn't have dared, had I not distinctly heard Neugebauer's crowing voice —

HANS KARL
He just left this very moment.

STANI
Otherwise I'd never have — because five minutes ago the new servant ran after me in the corridor, saying that you had Antoinette Hechingen's maid with you and would hardly be at home to anyone.

HANS KARL *half aloud*
Ah, he said that to you did he — charming fellow!

STANI
In that case, of course, I would under no circumstances have —

HANS KARL
She just returned a few books.

STANI
Toinette Hechingen reads books?

HANS KARL
Seems so. A couple of old French things.

STANI
From the eighteenth century. That matches her furniture.

HANS KARL *is silent.*

STANI
Her boudoir is charming. The little chaise longue. It's signed.

HANS KARL
Yes; the little chaise longue. Riesener.

STANI
Yes, Riesener. What a memory you have for names! The signature is low down.

HANS KARL
Yes, down at the lower end.

STANI
She always loses the little combs from her hair, and when one bends down to look for them one sees the inscription.

HANS KARL *walks over to the right and closes the door to the library.*

STANI
Do you feel a draught? Are you that susceptible?

HANS KARL
Yes, my riflemen and I, we got rheumatic out there, just like old hunting dogs.

STANI
You know, she speaks quite charmingly of you, Antoinette does.

HANS KARL *smokes*
Ah! …

STANI
No, but quite exceptionally so. I certainly owe the beginnings of any chance I had with her to the fact that she finds me so fabulously like you. For instance, our hands. She's ecstatic about your hands. *He examines his own hand.* But please don't mention a word of all this to Mama. It's just an all-out flirt, but then not a proper fling either. But Mama always gets things out of proportion.

HANS KARL
But my dear Stani, what could bring me to mention the subject?

STANI
Slowly but surely, she has of course, tumbled to the distinctions between us. *Ça va sans dire.*

HANS KARL
Antoinette has?

STANI
She described to me just how the friendship between you began.

HANS KARL
I have known her for ages, of course.

STANI
No, but this was two years ago. In the second year of the war. When you were on leave after your first wounding; those few days in Grünleiten.

HANS KARL
Does she date our friendship from that time?

STANI
Of course. Since then you are her special friend. As adviser, as confidant, as what you will; simply a cut above. She said you behaved like an angel.

HANS KARL
She's apt to exaggerate, our dear Antoinette.

STANI
But she told me down to the last detail how, fearing she would be left alone with her husband in Grünleiten, (he also happened to be on leave then) she asked Feri Uhlfeldt, who was chasing her for all he was worth at the time, to join her the next day; how she then sees you at the theatre the previous evening, and how in a burst of inspiration she asks you to drive out with her that same evening so as to spend it with herself and Adolf as a threesome.

HANS KARL
At that time I had scarcely got to know him.

STANI
Yes, and that, by the way is something she simply cannot grasp! That you should later have got so involved with him. With that dreary dunderhead, that pedant!

HANS KARL
There she does her husband a great injustice!

STANI
Ah well, I'm not going to get involved in any of that. But she tells it with such charm.

HANS KARL
That is indeed her strong point; all those little confidences.

STANI
Yes, that's how she begins. That whole evening — I can see it now — how she shows you round the garden after dinner; those charming terraces by the stream; how the moon rises …

HANS KARL
Ah, so she told you all of this in such detail.

STANI
And how during one notable nocturnal conversation, you had the strength to talk her out of having any further dealings with that Feri Uhlfeldt.

HANS KARL *smokes and is silent.*

STANI
That's what I so much admire about you: you say so little, are so detached, and yet have such presence. For that reason I find the topic which causes endless wagging of tongues perfectly normal: that you've held your seat in the Upper House this eighteen months, but never choose to speak. A gentleman such as you in fact speaks through his person! Oh, I've been studying you closely! In a couple more years I'll be there! At present I still have too much passion inside me. You never fully address anything and are not in the least verbose; that's what is so elegant about you. Anyone else in your position would have become her lover.

HANS KARL *with a smile noticeable only in his eyes*
You think so?

STANI
Without a doubt. But of course I understand perfectly: at your time of life you're too serious for all that. It no longer entices you: that's how I see it. You know, that's how I'm made: I think about everything. Had I had the time to stay on at university, science would have been my subject. I'd hit upon things, on problems, questions, which others don't even brush. For me, life without reflective thinking just isn't worth living. For instance: can one know, with a sudden jolt as it were, I am no longer a young man? — That must be a very unpleasant moment.

HANS KARL
You know, I believe it comes quite gradually. When someone else suddenly lets you pass through the door first and you then notice: yes of course, he's much younger, even though he too is already quite grown-up.

STANI
Most interesting. How well you observe everything. In that you're so like me. And then it simply forms into a habit, being older?

HANS KARL
Yes, there still remain certain moments that are striking. For example, when it suddenly becomes clear to one that one no longer believes there are people who could explain everything to one.

STANI
There's one thing I don't understand though, Uncle Kari, and that is: why is it, with your maturity and well-preserved as you are, that you don't marry?

HANS KARL
Right now?

STANI

Yes indeed, now. For you're simply no longer the sort of man who is looking for little adventures. You know, I'd understand at once, of course, that any woman might still be interested in you today. But Toinette explained to me why any interest you have never gets serious.

HANS KARL

Ah!

STANI

Yes, she's given it a lot of thought. She says: you never fasten onto anyone because you don't have enough heart.

HANS KARL

Ah!

STANI

Yes, you lack the essential component. That, she says, is the vast difference between you and me. She says, you always maintain a supple wrist, in order to let go. A woman can sense this, and even if she herself had been ready to fall in love with you, this prevents the process of crystallization.

HANS KARL

Ah, is that how she expresses it?

STANI

Yes, that's her great charm, that she commands the art of conversation. You know, I absolutely need that: a woman who fastens onto me must, apart from her complete devotion to me, also command conversation.

HANS KARL

In that she is quite delightful.

STANI

Absolutely. She has all of that: charm, wit and temperament, just as she lacks something else — namely breeding.

HANS KARL

You think so?

STANI

You know, Uncle Kari, I'm nothing if not just; however much a woman may have given proof of her regard for me, I return measure for measure, and I can see with remorseless clarity what she lacks. You understand what I'm saying: I think everything over and always create two categories. Thus I divide women into two major categories: the mistress and the woman one marries. Antoinette belongs to the first category; she can be Adolf Hechingen's wife a hundred times over, to my mind she's not a wife but rather — the other thing.

HANS KARL

That is her genre, of course. If one so wishes to pigeonhole people.

STANI

Absolutely, That is why, by the way, it's sheer futility wanting to reconcile her with her husband.

HANS KARL

But if he happens to be her husband for all that? Forgive me, that might possibly seem a very petit-bourgeois notion.

STANI

You know, forgive me, but I make my own categories and then I'm quite adamant on the subject, likewise on courtship, likewise on marriage. Marriage is not an experiment. It is the result of a correct decision.

HANS KARL

From which you are, of course, far removed.

STANI

Not in the least. Ready at any moment to make it.

HANS KARL

At this very moment?

STANI

I find myself exceptionally equipped to make a woman happy. But please don't let Mama know of this. I wish to preserve my complete freedom in all matters. In that I am like you to a hair. I cannot endure being restricted.

HANS KARL *smokes.*

STANI

A decision must be born of the moment. Now or not at all, that's my motto!

HANS KARL

Nothing in the world interests me so much as how anyone gets from one thing to the next. You would never keep postponing a decision then?

STANI

Never. That is absolute weakness.

HANS KARL

But surely there is such a thing as complications?

STANI

These I deny.

HANS KARL

For example, a clash of contradictory obligations.

STANI
One has a choice as to which of them should be resolved.

HANS KARL
But surely one is at times very much restricted in one's choice.

STANI
How come?

HANS KARL
Let's say, because of self-reproach.

STANI
Mere attacks of hypochondria. I'm perfectly healthy. Out in the field I wasn't sick a single day.

HANS KARL
Ah, so you're always absolutely content with your own behaviour?

STANI
Yes, if I weren't, I would certainly have behaved otherwise.

HANS KARL
Pardon me, I'm not referring to small misdemeanors — so, in a word, you'd allow chance, or let's call it destiny, to rule, without further thought.

STANI
How come? I always keep everything firmly in hand.

HANS KARL
At such times of decision one is nonetheless tempted to introduce a bizarre notion: that of a higher necessity.

STANI
Whatever I do just is necessary, otherwise I wouldn't do it.

HANS KARL *interested*
Forgive me if I draw my example from the actual present — it is not, in point of fact, quite the done thing —

STANI
Oh, please …

HANS KARL
A given situation would, let us say, hasten your decision to marry.

STANI
Today, tomorrow, or the next day.

HANS KARL
Now you are after all, friends with Antoinette in this way.

STANI
I would quarrel and fall out with her from one day to the next!

HANS KARL
Ah! Without the slightest grounds?

STANI
But good grounds are never far to seek. I ask you. Our relationship has held since last year. For the past six or seven weeks there is something about Antoinette, I can't say what — a suspicion would be going too far — but the very idea that she might have her mind on someone else besides me; you know, I'm quite adamant there.

HANS KARL
Ah, indeed.

STANI
You know, that's more than I can take. I don't even wish to call it jealousy; it's something quite inconceivable that a woman to whom I have become attached could at the same time give another — you know what I mean?

HANS KARL
But Antoinette is such an innocent if she's been up to something. She then almost possesses even greater charm.

STANI
I don't follow you there.

SCENE NINE

NEUGEBAUER *has come in quietly*
Here are the letters, your Lordship. I managed, at the first attempt —

HANS KARL
Thank you. Please hand them to me.

NEUGEBAUER *hands him the letters.*

HANS KARL
Thank you.

Exit NEUGEBAUER.

SCENE TEN

HANS KARL *after a short pause*
You know who I consider to be the born husband?

STANI
Well?

HANS KARL
Adolf Hechingen.

STANI
That husband of Antoinette's! Hahaha!

HANS KARL
I'm pefectly serious in what I say.

STANI
But Uncle Kari.

HANS KARL
There is, in his attachment to this woman, something of a higher necessity.

STANI
That predestined — I won't say what.

HANS KARL
His destiny matters to me.

STANI
In my book he belongs in a particular category: a man without instinct. Do you know to whom he attaches himself when you aren't at the club? To me! To me of all people! Has he got a nose for things!

HANS KARL
I like him a lot.

STANI
But he's uncouth to the tips of his ears.

HANS KARL
But an inwardly noble man.

STANI
An uncouth, hamfisted fellow.

HANS KARL
All he needs is a bottle of champagne in his blood.

STANI
Never say that in front of him or he'll take you at your word. An uncouth fellow is
an abomination to me when he's had a drink.

HANS KARL
I like him a lot.

STANI
He takes everything literally, including your friendship for him.

HANS KARL
But he's perfectly welcome to take that literally.

STANI
Sorry, Uncle Kari, but with you nothing may be taken literally. If one does that, one
falls into the category: no instinct.

HANS KARL
But he is such a good, valuable human being.

STANI
As you please, if you say so of him; but that still gives him no proper cause to keep
mentioning your goodness. That really gets on my nerves. A well-bred person has
bonhomie, but he's not a good person. Excuse me, I say: my Uncle Kari is a great
gentleman and therefore a great egoist too, that's obvious. Forgive my saying so.

HANS KARL
It's no good; I like him a lot.

STANI
That's just quirkiness on your part! And surely you've no need to be quirky! After
all, you have that splendid gift of effortlessly being exactly what you are: a great
gentleman! Effortlessly! That's the whole point. A person of a lower category exerts
himself endlessly. Witness our friend Theophil Neuhoff, who for the past year may
be seen everywhere. What else is such a creature but an ongoing, abject endeavour
to ape a style which happens not to be his style.

SCENE ELEVEN

LUKE *comes in hurriedly*
May I enquire — did your Lordship give instructions for non-family visitors to be
admitted?

HANS KARL
Absolutely not. What is it then?

LUKE
Then the new servant must have confused matters. The hall porter has just telephoned upstairs that Baron Neuhoff is on the stairs. May I enquire, what's to be done with him.

STANI
Well, just the very moment we're talking of him. That's no accident. Uncle Kari, that man is my bugbear and I've conjured up his appearance. A week ago at Helen's place, I was just about to offer my opinion on Herr von Neuhoff, and in that instant Neuhoff stood on the threshold. Three days ago, as I was leaving Antoinette — there in the hall stands Herr von Neuhoff. Yesterday morning at my mother's — I urgently needed to discuss something with her — I find Herr von Neuhoff in the hall.

VINCENT *enters, announces*
Baron Neuhoff is in the hall.

LUKE *makes a sign: to be admitted.*

VINCENT *opens the double door, ushers him in.*

SCENE TWELVE

NEUHOFF *steps in*
Good evening, Count Bühl. I made so bold as to find out whether you were at home.

HANS KARL
You are acquainted with my nephew Freudenberg?

NEUHOFF
We have met. *They sit down.*

NEUHOFF
I was to have had the pleasure of meeting you this evening at the Altenwyls' house. Countess Helen had been looking forward a little to make us acquainted. The more acute was my regret when I learnt from Countess Helen this afternoon, that you had turned down the invitation.

HANS KARL
You have known my cousin since last winter?

NEUHOFF
Known — if one may indeed use the word of such a being. At certain moments one may but realize how ambiguous that word is: it designates the most superficial thing in the world and then the deepest mystery of existence between one human being and another.

HANS KARL *and* STANI *exchange glances.*

NEUHOFF

I have the great fortune of not infrequently meeting Countess Helen and of being bound in devotion to her.

A small, somewhat embarrassed pause.

NEUHOFF

This afternoon — we were together in Bohuslawsky's studio — Bohuslawsky is painting my portrait, or rather, he is going through the utmost torments in attempting to capture the expression of my eyes: he speaks of a certain quality visible there only at rare moments — and it was his wish that Countess Helen should view this picture and offer her judgement of these eyes — then she said to me: Count Bühl is not coming, do go to see him. Simply pay him a visit. He is a man with whom nature and truth may attain anything, yet mere intention, nothing. A wonderful man in our intention-filled world, was my reply — and that is how I imagined him to be, that is how I suspected him to be at our first meeting.

STANI

You met my uncle in the field?

NEUHOFF

Amongst staff officers.

HANS KARL

Not in the most agreeable company.

NEUHOFF

That was evident from your manner; you hardly uttered a word.

HANS KARL

I'm no great talker; isn't that right, Stani?

STANI

In private company, you are.

NEUHOFF

You say it all, Count Freudenberg; your uncle loves to pay in gold coin; he has felt disinclined to adapt to the paper money of daily discourse. By speaking he can only give up his private self, and that is beyond price.

HANS KARL

You are too kind, Baron Neuhoff.

NEUHOFF

You really ought to allow Bohuslawsky to paint you, Count Bühl. With you he would hit the mark in three sittings. You know that his forte is child portraiture. Your smile has precisely that hint of a child's radiant face. Don't misunderstand me. Why is dignity so inimitable? Because it contains a suggestion of the childlike. By way of that childlike quality, Bohuslawsky would be able to lend a portrait of you that rarest of things in our world which so distinguishes your appearance: dignity. For we live in a world without dignity.

HANS KARL
I don't know which world you are referring to: all of us encountered so much dignity out there —

NEUHOFF
That is why a man such as yourself was so much in his element out there. What did you not achieve, Count Bühl! I recall the NCO in hospital who was buried alive with you and thirty other riflemen.

HANS KARL
My brave platoon sergeant, poor Franz! My cousin told you about it, did she?

NEUHOFF
She permitted me to accompany her to the hospital for this visit. Never shall I forget either the face or the words of this dying man.

HANS KARL *says nothing.*

NEUHOFF
He spoke of no one but yourself. And in what tone of voice! He knew that the woman he was speaking to was a relative of his captain.

HANS KARL
My poor Franz!

NEUHOFF
Perhaps the Countess Helen wished to give me some sense of your nature, such as a thousand meetings in a drawing-room could never convey.

STANI *somewhat sharply*
Perhaps she wished above all to see the man himself and to hear news of Uncle Kari.

NEUHOFF
In a situation such as this, a being like Helen Altenwyl can only become her true self. Beneath this utter simplicity, this pride of good breeding, lies hidden a surging love, a feeling of sympathy which permeates every pore: there are between her and the being she loves and respects, bonds which nothing could sever and nothing may touch. Woe betide the husband who should fail to honour this secret bond of intimacy within her, or who was petty enough to wish that all these dispersed sympathies be joined solely in his person.

A brief pause.

HANS KARL *smokes.*

NEUHOFF

She is like you: one of those beings whose favour cannot be courted: who must surrender of their own accord.

Again a brief pause.

NEUHOFF *with great, but perhaps not quite genuine assurance*

I am a wanderer, I have been driven by curiosity half way round the globe. Whatever is hard to apprehend, fascinates me. I would wish to see a proud, precious being such as Countess Helen in company with you, Count Bühl. She would become transformed, she would blossom; for I know no one quite so sensitive to human quality.

HANS KARL

All of us here have a little of that. This is perhaps nothing quite so special about my cousin.

NEUHOFF

I imagine the society fit to hold a being like Helen Altenwyl, as consisting only of men of your calibre. Every culture has its flowering: real content without any pretention, nobility tempered by infinite gracefulness, that is what the flower of this ancient society consists of; a society that has succeeded where the ruins of Luxor and the forests of the Caucasus had failed; namely, in holding a restless spirit such as myself in their spell. But do explain one thing to me, Count Bühl. Why is it that men of your stamp especially, from whom society acquires its essential character, are all too rarely met there? They appear to avoid it.

STANI

But by no means, you shall see Uncle Kari at the Altenwyls' this very evening, and I even fear that, however cosy our little chat here is, we must soon give him the chance to get changed.

He has risen to his feet.

NEUHOFF

If we must do so, I'll say goodbye to you for the present, Count Bühl. Should you at any time, whatever the situation, require the services of a knight errant, *already on his way*, who is willing, wherever he senses the noble and the exalted, to serve this wholeheartedly and reverently, then call upon me.

HANS KARL *followed by* STANI *accompany him. When they reach the door, the telephone rings.*

NEUHOFF

Please stay, the appliance demands your attention.

STANI

May I escort you to the stairs?

HANS KARL *by the door*
I thank you for your kind visit, Baron Neuhoff.

NEUHOFF *and* STANI *leave.*

HANS KARL *alone with the persistently ringing telephone, goes over to the wall and presses the internal communication bell, calling out:*
Luke, turn it off! I don't like this indiscreet contraption! Luke!

The ringing stops.

SCENE THIRTEEN

STANI *returns*
Just for a second, Uncle Kari, if you'll forgive me. I simply had to hear your verdict on that gentleman!

HANS KARL
Yours appears to be cut and dried.

STANI
Ah, I find him simply impossible. I simply don't understand such a figure. And then the fellow is quite well-born.

HANS KARL
And you find him that unacceptable?

STANI
Well I ask you: as many *faux pas* as words uttered.

HANS KARL
He wishes to be agreeable; he wants to win others over.

STANI
But surely one has some self-respect, one doesn't shamelessly thrust oneself upon total strangers.

HANS KARL
And indeed he believes one can try to be something special — that I would consider a form of naivety or an error in upbringing.

STANI *walks up and down in agitation*
Those tirades all about Helen!

HANS KARL
That a girl like Helen holds converstions with him about ourselves doesn't appeal to me either.

STANI

There's certainly not a word of truth in all that. A chap who blows hot and cold from the same mouth.

HANS KARL

It will have been very much as he says. Yet there are people in whose mouth all nuances tend to be altered, quite involuntarily.

STANI

You possess a vast measure of tolerance!

HANS KARL

It's just that I'm very old, Stani.

STANI

I, at any rate, am livid; the whole thing brings me to the boil; this pretence at assurance, this oily smooth talk, this coquettish playing with his odious little beard.

HANS KARL

He has intellect, yet it somehow makes one feel uncomfortable.

STANI

These unmentionable indiscretions. I ask you: what has your face got to do with him?

HANS KARL

At bottom, one is possibly a person to be pitied if one is made like that.

STANI

I say he's an odious fellow. But now I must go up to Mama. I shall at all events see you at the club tonight, Uncle Kari.

AGATHA *quietly peeps in at the door; she thinks* HANS KARL *is alone.* STANI *comes forward once more.* HANS KARL *signs to* AGATHA *to disappear.*

STANI

You know, I just can't calm down. First the downright shabbiness of flattering a gentleman such as you to his face.

HANS KARL

That was not very elegant.

STANI

Secondly, parading his oh-so-close friendship with Helen. Thirdly, his sleuthing about to see whether you were interested in her.

HANS KARL *smiling*

Do you think that he wanted to sound out the territory a little?

STANI

Fourthly, that appallingly indiscreet allusion as to his future station. He presented himself in so many words as her husband to be. Fifthly, that odious speechifying which makes it impossible for me to return the compliment even once. Sixthly, that impossible exit speech. That was nothing short of a birthday address, a leading article. But I'm holding you up, Uncle Kari.

AGATHA *has appeared again in the doorway. The same routine as earlier.*

STANI *on the point of disappearing, comes forward once more*
Might I, for one last time? There's one thing I fail to grasp and that is, why all this business about Helen doesn't concern you more!

HANS KARL
Why me exactly?

STANI
Forgive me, but I'm too close to Helen myself to be able to savour this ridiculous phrase "devotion" and "bound". Especially when I've known Helen like a sister from the time she was little!

HANS KARL
There comes a time when sisters and brothers go their separate ways.

STANI
But not for the sake of a Neuhoff. Oh, dear me, no!

HANS KARL
A tiny dose of untruth is most agreeable to women.

STANI
A fellow like him shouldn't be allowed near her!

HANS KARL
We won't be able to prevent it.

STANI
Oh, I'd like to see that! Nowhere near her!

HANS KARL
He has made known his future relationship to us.

STANI
What state of mind must Helen be in, if she gets involved with this type.

HANS KARL
You know, I've rather lost the habit of drawing conclusions, from any actions taken by women about their state of mind.

STANI

Not that I'm at all jealous, mind, but to imagine a person like Helen — as the wife of this Neuhoff; to me that's such an inconceivable notion — the very idea is beyond me — I must speak to Mama about it at once.

HANS KARL *smiling*
Yes indeed, do just that, Stani. —

Exit STANI.

SCENE FOURTEEN

LUKE *enters*
I fear the telephone call was put through directly.

HANS KARL
I won't have that.

LUKE
Very well, your Lordship. The new servant must have redirected the call without my noticing. He has his hands and ears everywhere they are not supposed to be.

HANS KARL
Tomorrow morning at seven sharp, send him packing.

LUKE
Very good. Count Hechingen's servant was on the line. The count personally wishes to speak about this evening: whether your Lordship is attending the soiree at Count Altenwyl's or not. That is, since her Ladyship the Countess will also be there.

HANS KARL
Call up the Altenwyls' place to say that I have made myself free and ask if I may be permitted to appear despite having cancelled. And then connect me with Count Hechingen: I'll speak to him myself. And meanwhile ask the lady's maid to come in.

LUKE
Very well. *Exit.* AGATHA *enters.*

SCENE FIFTEEN

HANS KARL *takes up the packet of letters*
Here are the letters. Tell my lady Countess that I can part with these letters only because the memory of all that was beautiful, to me remains imperishable; I shall not find it in a letter, but everywhere.

AGATHA
Oh, I'm ever so grateful! I'm so very happy. Now I know that her Ladyship will soon be seeing our dear Count again.

HANS KARL
She shall see me this evening. I shall be coming to the soiree.

AGATHA
And are we to hope that you — that the man who stands before her will be the same man as ever?

HANS KARL
She has no better friend.

AGATHA
Oh, I'm ever so grateful!

HANS KARL
She has only two real friends in the world: me and her husband.

AGATHA
Oh, Lord, I don't wish to hear that. Heavens, what misfortune that our dear Count has formed a friendship with Count Hechingen. My Lady Countess is truly spared nothing.

HANS KARL *nervously takes a few paces away from her*
Do women really have so little idea of what a husband is?! And who it is that truly loves them?

AGATHA
Oh, anything but that. We're prepared to be persuaded of anything by your Lordship, other than that; that's just too much!

HANS KARL *walking up and down*
So that's out! Can't be of any help! Not of the slightest! *Pause.*

AGATHA *shyly stepping closer to him*
But do try all the same. Only not through me: I'm too uneducated for such a message. I wouldn't find the right expressions there. And not by letter either. That only leads to misunderstandings. But eye to eye: yes, that's it! Then you'll make headway! And what couldn't you achieve with my Mistress! Perhaps not at first attempt. But by repetition — if you really addressed her conscience insistently — how could she ever resist you then? *The telephone rings once again.*

HANS KARL *goes over to the telephone and speaks into it*
Yes, speaking. Here. Count Bühl. Yes, in person.

AGATHA
I'll say goodbye. *Leaves rapidly via centre door.*

HANS KARL *on the telephone*
Hechingen, good evening! Yes, I had second thoughts. I have accepted. I shall look for an opportunity. Certainly. Yes, that persuaded me to go. Especially at a soiree, since I don't play Bridge and your wife doesn't either, I believe. Don't mention it. No need for that either. For your pessimism. For your pessimism! You don't understand? There's no call for your dejection. Fight, at all costs! On your own? The famous bottle of champagne then. I shall certainly come with a result before midnight. No excessive hopes either, of course. You know that I'll attempt all that's humanly possible. That also accords with my sentiments. It accords with my sentiments! What's that? Interference? I said: it accords with my sentiments. Sentiments! A perfectly trivial phrase! Not a phase, a phrase! I said, a trivial phrase. Which? That it accords with my sentiments. No, I merely call it a trivial phrase, because you failed to understand it all this time. Yes. Yes indeed! Cheerio. Full stop! *Rings off.* There are people with whom everything gets complicated, and yet he's such an excellent chap!

SCENE SIXTEEN

STANI *once again in the centre doorway*
Am I being a perfect pest, Uncle Kari?

HANS KARL
But of course not. I'm at your disposal.

STANI *to the fore, next to him*
I must let you know, Uncle Kari, that I have in the meantime had a conversation with Mama, and have come to a conclusion.

HANS KARL *looks at him.*

STANI
I shall become engaged to Helen Altenwyl.

HANS KARL
You'll become —

STANI
Yes, I am determined to marry Helen. Not today or tomorrow, but at earliest opportunity. I've thought everything through. On the staircase between here and the second floor. When I got to Mama on the second floor, everything was cut and dried. You see, the idea suddenly came to me when I noticed that you had no interest in Helen.

HANS KARL
Aha.

STANI

Don't you see? It was just an idea of Mama's. She maintains that one never knows where one stands with you — in the end you might well have hit on the idea of claiming Helen after all — and for Mama you remain the head of the family; her heart, after all, is wholly that of a Bühl.

HANS KARL *half turned away*
Dear old Crescence!

STANI

But I kept contradicting her. I do so understand every nuance about you. I have always felt that there couldn't be a single jot of interest in Helen on your part.

HANS KARL *suddenly turns round to face him*
And your mother?

STANI
Mama?

HANS KARL
Yes, how did she see it?

STANI

Aflame with enthusiasm, of course. She flushed bright red with joy. Are you surprised, Uncle Kari?

HANS KARL

A tiny bit, just a wee hint — I have always been under the impression that your mother held to one specific notion in regard to Helen.

STANI
An aversion?

HANS KARL
By no means. Merely a view. A supposition.

STANI
Earlier, in years gone by?

HANS KARL
No: half an hour ago.

STANI

In what direction? But Mama really is such a weather-vane! She forgets things in an instant. Faced with a decision of mine, she's down on her knees at once. That's where she senses the man. She worships the *fait accompli*.

HANS KARL
So you've made your decision then? —

STANI
Yes, my mind's made up.

HANS KARL
Just like that, at a stroke!

STANI
But that's exactly what it's all about. That's what so greatly impresses women about me. In that way I always keep the initiative firmly in hand.

HANS KARL *smokes.*

STANI
You see, at one time you might also have thought of marrying Helen yourself ...

HANS KARL
Good Lord, many years ago perhaps. At some odd moment or other, just as one thinks of a thousand other matters.

STANI
Don't you see? I've never even thought about it! But the instant I do think it, I see it through. You're out of sorts?

HANS KARL
I quite involuntarily let my thoughts go out to Antoinette for a moment.

STANI
But every single thing on earth must come to an end eventually.

HANS KARL
Naturally. And you're not at all exercised as to whether Helen is free or not? She seems, for instance, to have given our friend Neuhoff some hope.

STANI
But that's exactly my calculation. Any hopes Herr von Neuhoff might have, I shall simply pass over. And that a man such as Theophil Neuhoff could even remotely be considered as Helen's suitor, is surely clear proof of the fact that there can be no such thing for her as serious occupation of territory. I can't detect any such complications. Those are merely whims or let's call it: aberrations.

HANS KARL
She's difficult to know.

STANI
But I do know her precise type. In the last resort she cannot become interested in any type of man other than ours; everything else is an aberration. You're so quiet; have you your headache?

HANS KARL
Not in the least. I admire your courage.

STANI
Admire courage — you of all people?

HANS KARL
This is another kind of courage than in the trenches.

STANI
Yes, I understand you perfectly, Uncle Kari. You're thinking of all the opportunities I might have had in life. You have the feeling that I might possibly be putting too low a price on myself. But don't you see, I'm quite different there: I love what's rational and definite. You, Uncle Kari are, at bottom, if you'll pardon my frankness, an idealist: your thoughts are directed at the absolute, at perfection. That's all very elegant in conception, but never to be realized. You are, at bottom, rather like Mama there; in her eyes nothing is good enough for me. I've thought the matter through for what it's worth. Helen is a year younger than me.

HANS KARL
A year?

STANI
She is extremely well born.

HANS KARL
None better.

STANI
She is elegant.

HANS KARL
Very elegant.

STANI
She's rich.

HANS KARL
And above all so pretty.

STANI
She has breeding.

HANS KARL
Beyond comparison.

STANI
Now, above all, regarding the two points which really do matter in marriage. First: she cannot tell a lie; second: she has the best manners in the world.

HANS KARL
She is so delightfully well-mannered, such as only elderly ladies are.

STANI
She's as bright as the day is long.

HANS KARL
Who are you telling? I do so love her conversation.

STANI
And given time, she will simply adore me.

HANS KARL *to himself, involuntarily*
That too is possible.

STANI
Not just possible. Quite certain. With this type of woman, it all follows in consequence of marriage. In a liaison everything depends on circumstance; bizarre interludes may occur, deceptions, God knows what else besides. In marriage everything rests on permanence; in the long term each party so far takes over the essence of the other, that there can be no more question of any real difference. Under the one proviso: that the marriage results from making the correct decision. That is the meaning of marriage.

SCENE SEVENTEEN

LUKE *entering*
The Countess Freudenberg.

CRESCENCE *walking past* LUKE; *steps in quickly*
Well now, what do you have to say about my boy, Kari? I'm simply overjoyed. You must congratulate me!

HANS KARL *somewhat absent-minded*
My dear Crescence. My best wishes for every success.

STANI *takes his leave without a word.*

CRESCENCE
Do have the car sent for me.

STANI
It's at your disposal. I'll be going on foot. *Exit.*

SCENE EIGHTEEN

CRESCENCE
Success will very much depend on you.

HANS KARL
On me? Surely it's written all over him that he succeeds at whatever he turns his hand to.

CRESCENCE
For Helen, your judgement means everything.

HANS KARL
How do you mean, Crescence, in what way?

CRESCENCE
For her father Altenwyl even more so, of course. Our Stani is a very tolerable match, but not exactly stunning. I don't have any illusions about that. But if you gave him your support, Kari; just a word from you carries so much weight with the old couple. I can't think what the reason might be.

HANS KARL
I just about belong to them myself, I should say.

CRESCENCE
Don't you get coquettish about your age. We two are neither old nor young. But I detest a fuzzy state of affairs. In that event I'd rather be left sitting there with grey hair and horn-rimmed spectacles.

HANS KARL
That's why you're losing no time in match-making.

CRESCENCE
I've always wanted to help you there, Kari, even twelve years ago. But you always maintained that quiet, obstinate resistance inside you.

HANS KARL
My dear good Crescence!

CRESCENCE
I've told you a hundred times: let me know what you're after, and I'll take it in hand.

HANS KARL
Yes, that's what you often told me, goodness knows, Crescence.

CRESCENCE
But then one couldn't ever be sure where one stood with you!

HANS KARL *nods.*

CRESCENCE

So now our Stani is about to do what you didn't want to do. I simply can't wait to see little children running about in Hohenbühl and in Göllersdorf.

HANS KARL

And to fall into the castle pond! Don't you remember how they pulled me out half dead? You know — I sometimes get the idea that nothing new ever happens in life.

CRESCENCE

How do you mean?

HANS KARL

That everything has long since been laid up for us somewhere, and only becomes visible of a sudden. You know, like in the pond at Hohenbühl when they let out all the water in autumn: and the carp and the tails of the stone Tritons, which one hardly ever saw, suddenly come into view? A fanciful idea, what!

CRESCENCE

Are you not quite yourself all of a sudden, Kari?

HANS KARL *gives himself a little jolt*

On the contrary, Crescence, I thank you most sincerely, both you and Stani, for the brisk tempo you impart to me with all your sparkle and your decisiveness. *He kisses her hand.*

CRESCENCE

Do you find it does you good, having us about you?

HANS KARL

I now have a most agreeable evening before me. First a serious conversation with Toinette —

CRESCENCE

But we won't be needing that at all now!

HANS KARL

Ah, but I shall have a word with her, now that I've made up my mind to do so. And then I'm supposed to conduct certain earnest exchanges as Stani's uncle.

CRESCENCE

The chief point is that you set him in a favourable light in Helen's eyes.

HANS KARL

Well, that certainly provides me with a definite programme. You see how you are reforming me? But you know, before that — I have an idea — before that I'll go to the circus for an hour. They have a clown there now — a sort of funny man —

CRESCENCE
That's Furlani; Nanni is quite crazy about him. I don't have much time for such pranks myself.

HANS KARL
I find him quite delightful. He entertains me far more than the cleverest conversation with God knows whom. I'll go to the circus, have a bite to eat in a restaurant, and then I'll arrive at the soiree in good form to complete my programme.

CRESCENCE
Indeed, you'll come and play Stani right into Helen's hands: you can handle that sort of thing so nicely. You might have made such a splendid ambassador, if you'd only wanted to remain in that career.

HANS KARL
It's a bit late for all that as well.

CRESCENCE
Well then amuse yourself thoroughly and follow on soon.

HANS KARL *accompanies her to the door. Exit* CRESCENCE.

SCENE NINETEEN

HANS KARL *comes forward.* LUKE *has entered with him.*

HANS KARL
I shall wear tails. I'll ring presently.

LUKE
Very well, your Lordship.

HANS KARL *exit left.*

SCENE TWENTY

VINCENT *steps in from the right*
What are you up to there?

LUKE
I'm waiting for the bell to ring in the dressing room: I shall then go in to help.

VINCENT
I'll go in too. It's a good idea if I start getting used to him.

LUKE
No such orders have been given, so you will remain outside.

VINCENT *helps himself to a cigar*
Tell me, he's quite a simple, friendly sort, isn't he? Those relatives do what they like with him, right? In a month I'll have him twisted round my little finger.

LUKE *locks up the cigars. A bell is heard.* LUKE *hurries on.*

VINCENT
Take your time. Let him ring twice. *Sits down in an armchair.*

Exit LUKE *behind him.*

VINCENT *to himself*
He hands back his love letters, he's marrying off his nephew, and he's made up his mind to spend his days as an ageing bachelor with me. That's just how I imagined things would be.

Over his shoulder backwards, without turning round Hey, Squire, I'm quite happy here, I'll stay!

The curtain falls.

ACT TWO

At the Altenwyls'. Small living room furnished in eighteenth-century style. Doors left, right and centre. ALTENWYL *enters right with* HANS KARL. CRESCENCE *with* HELEN *and* NEUHOFF *stand left conversing.*

SCENE ONE

ALTENWYL
My dear Kari, I appreciate your coming more than ever, since you don't play Bridge and so are happy to make do with such modest fragments of drawing-room conversation as may still be afforded one these days. You will, as you know, only find the same familiar old faces, no artists or other celebrities — true, Edine Merenburg is extremely unhappy with this old-fashioned way of running a household, yet neither Helen nor I savour that species of socializing which for Edine is the height of perfection: where she can quizz the person next to her at table before the first spoonful of soup, as to whether he believes in the transmigration of souls or if he had ever drunk friendship with a fakir.

CRESCENCE
There I must correct you, Count Altenwyl; I see a completely new face over there at my Bridge table, and as Mariette Stradonitz whispered in my ear, it's a world-famous scholar of whom we have never even heard, simply because we are quite illiterate.

ALTENWYL
Professor Brücke is a great celebrity in his field and to me a welcome political colleague. He greatly enjoys being in a salon where he won't find any colleague from the world of learning, being, so to speak, the sole representative of intellect in a purely social environment; and since my house is able to afford him this modest amenity —

CRESCENCE
Is he married?

ALTENWYL
I, at any rate, have never had the honour of coming face to face with any Madame Brücke.

CRESCENCE
I find famous men quite odious, but their wives more dreadful still. In this I'm of one mind with Kari. We adore trivial people and trivial conversation, isn't that so, Kari?

ALTENWYL
I have my own old-fashioned view of the matter, well known to Helen.

CRESCENCE
Kari must say that he agrees with me. I find that nine-tenths of all that goes by the name of intellect is nothing but small-talk.

NEUHOFF *to* **HELEN**
Are you also that severe, Countess Helen?

HELEN
Those of us who belong to the younger generation have every reason to feel appalled by at least one thing, and it is this: that there should be something called 'conversation'; words which reduce to banality everything that is real and make a sedative out of small-talk.

CRESCENCE
Do say that you agree with me, Kari!

HANS KARL
I beg your indulgence. Furlani is no sort of preparation for saying something clever.

ALTENWYL
In my view, conversation is just what nobody today knows much about: not spouting away like a waterfall oneself, but giving the cue to another. In my day it used to be said: if someone comes to my place I must so conduct conversation with him that if he thinks himself brilliant when his hand is on the door-knob, then he'll find me brilliant on the staircase. — But nowadays, no one, if you'll pardon my bluntness, possesses the skill of making conversation, and no one, that of keeping his mouth shut — ah, permit me to introduce you to Baron Neuhoff: my cousin, Count Bühl.

NEUHOFF
I have the honour of already being known to Count Bühl.

CRESCENCE *to* **ALTENWYL**
You must say all these clever things to Edine — for her the cult of important people and everything in print knows no bounds. To me, the very word 'important people' is odious — there's such total *presumption* in the term!

ALTENWYL
Edine is a very clever woman but she always tries to kill two birds with one stone: to increase her level of education and to reap some benefit for her charity-mongering.

HELEN
Forgive me, Papa, but she is not a clever woman, she's a stupid woman who relishes nothing so much as to surround herself with clever people, yet always manages to pick on the wrong ones.

CRESCENCE
I only wonder that, given her chronic absent-mindedness, she doesn't generate even more confusion.

ALTENWYL
Such beings have a guardian angel.

EDINE *joins them via the middle door*
I can see you're talking about me; just carry on, don't feel bashful.

CRESCENCE
Well, Edine, have you got to know the famous man yet?

EDINE
I'm furious, Count Altenwyl, that you have given him to her as partner and not to me.

Sits down by CRESCENCE.
You can't imagine how interested I am in him. I do read people's books, you know. Only a couple of weeks ago I read a fat volume by this man Brückner.

NEUHOFF
His name is Brücke. He is vice-president of the Academy of Sciences.

EDINE
In Paris?

NEUHOFF
No, here in Vienna.

EDINE
On the book it said: Brückner.

CRESCENCE
Perhaps that was a misprint.

EDINE
On the cover it said: 'On the Origin of all Religions'. It had such erudition and depth! And such a lovely style!

HELEN
I'll bring him over for you, Aunt Edine.

NEUHOFF
If you'll permit me, I'll look for him and bring him here; as soon as he has a break.

EDINE
Yes, please do so, Baron Neuhoff. Tell him that I've been on his trail for years.

NEUHOFF *exit left.*

CRESCENCE
He won't wish for anything better; it seems to me that he's rather a —

EDINE
Don't always rush in with "snob"; Goethe too had just about every Princess and Countess — now I almost said something —

CRESCENCE
Now she's off on Goethe again, old Edine! *Looks around for* HANS KARL *who has moved to the right with* HELEN.

HELEN *to* HANS KARL
You like him that much, Furlani, I mean?

HANS KARL
For me a person like that means true recreation.

HELEN
Does he do such clever tricks? *She sits down on the right,* HANS KARL *sits beside her.* CRESCENCE *exit through the centre.* ALTENWYL *and* EDINE *have sat down on the left.*

HANS KARL
He doesn't do any tricks. He's just the old-fashioned prankster!

HELEN
A clown then?

HANS KARL
No, that would be an exaggeration! He never exaggerates, neither does he caricature. He simply plays his role. He's the chap who wants to understand everybody, to help everybody, and yet in doing so brings about the utmost confusion. He performs the silliest pranks, the gallery rocks with laughter, while he maintains such poise, such discreetness; one sees that he respects himself as well as everything else in the world. He creates confusion, makes an unholy mess of things; wherever he goes everything is made topsy-turvy, and all the time one wants to shout: "but he's quite right!"

EDINE *to* ALTENWYL
The things of the mind give us women so much more support! That's something totally absent in Antoinette, for instance. I always say to her: she ought to cultivate her mind; that helps to take one's mind off other things.

ALTENWYL
In my day one used to judge conversation by quite another yardstick. One actually valued fine repartee; one had to put one's back into it if one wished to show brilliance.

EDINE
What I say is, when I make conversation, I wish to be led to new pastures; I wish to escape from banality. I wish to be transported somewhere!

HANS KARL *to* HELEN, *continuing his conversation*
You see, Helen, all these things happen to be difficult; these tricks by tight-rope walkers and jugglers — it all requires a phenomenal exertion of will and indeed intellect. I fancy, more intellect than for most conversations.

HELEN
Ah, too true.

HANS KARL
Absolutely. But what Furlani performs is a whole step above what others do. All the others let themselves be ruled by intention and look neither to right nor left; indeed, they hardly draw breath until they've achieved what they'd intended: that's the whole purpose of their trick. Yet he seemingly does nothing by intention — he always submits to that of others. He wants to do exactly what others do; he shows such readiness to please, is so fascinated by every little trick someone else performs. If he balances a flower-pot on his nose, he does so, as it were, out of sheer politeness.

HELEN
But he does drop it?

HANS KARL
Yes, but the way he drops it, therein lies the point! He drops it out of sheer exuberance and elation at the fact that he can so beautifully balance it! He thinks that if one pulls the thing off perfectly, it might all happen of its own accord.

HELEN *to herself*
And that's what the flower-pot usually can't take, and so falls to the ground.

ALTENWYL *to* EDINE
That cut-and-dried tone nowadays! I ask you, even between men and women: that element of purposiveness in all conversation!

EDINE
Yes, I have a horror of it too! Surely one wants to have things dressed up a little, a bit of hide-and-seek —

ALTENWYL
Young people no longer know that the sauce is worth twice as much as the roast — there's such an over-supply of directness!

EDINE
Simply because people have read far too little! Because they neglect to cultivate their minds!

They have got to their feet while talking and move off to the left.

HANS KARL *to* HELEN
When one observes that man Furlani, even the cleverest clowns seem vulgar. He is actually beautiful from sheer nonchalance — but of course this nonchalance demands exactly double the effort compared to all that strenuousness in others.

HELEN
I can well understand that you find this man appealing. I also find everything in which one can detect intention, a little vulgar.

HANS KARL
Oho, it so happens I'm crammed with intentions myself today, and these intentions have reference to you, Countess Helen.

HELEN *frowning a little*
Oh, Countess Helen! You're addressing me as "Countess Helen"?

HUBERTA *appears in the doorway and throws* HANS KARL *and* HELEN *a brief, but indiscreet glance.*

HANS KARL *without noticing* HUBERTA
No, but seriously, I must beg of you just five minutes' conversation — perhaps later sometime — since neither of us is playing.

HELEN *somewhat uneasy, yet very much in control*
You're making me alarmed. What can you wish to speak to me about? It can't be anything agreeable.

HANS KARL
If it should trouble you, then in heaven's name, no!

HUBERTA *has disappeared.*

HELEN *after a brief pause*
If you wish, but later. I see Huberta, who is looking bored. I must go over to her.

HANS KARL
You are so delightfully well-behaved. *He has also risen.*

HELEN
You must now go and pay your respects to Antoinette and the rest of the ladies. *She moves away from him but remains standing in the centre doorway.* I'm not well-behaved: I merely sense what goes on inside people, and that bothers me — and then I react with such civilities as I feel for people. My manners are just a form of nervous response to keep people at bay. *She leaves.*

HANS KARL *slowly follows her.*

SCENE TWO

NEUHOFF *and the* FAMOUS MAN *have appeared simultaneously in the left-hand doorway.*

FAMOUS MAN *having reached the centre of the room and looking through the right doorway*
Over there in the group by the fireplace, the lady whose name I wanted to ask you can now be seen.

NEUHOFF
Over there, in grey? That is the Princess Pergen.

FAMOUS MAN
No, I've known her for ages. The lady in black.

NEUHOFF
The Spanish ambassador's wife. Have you been presented to her? Or may I —

FAMOUS MAN
I would very much like to be presented to her. But we might contrive to do so in the following manner —

NEUHOFF *with scarcely perceptible irony*
Just as you command.

FAMOUS MAN
If you would be so kind, first to make mention of me to the lady, making clear to her, since she is a foreigner, my importance, my status in the world of learning and in society — I would then have Count Altenwyl present me to her immediately thereafter.

NEUHOFF
But of course, with the greatest pleasure.

FAMOUS MAN
It is not, for a scholar of my status, so much a matter of increasing my circle of acquaintances, as to be known and accepted in the appropriate manner.

NEUHOFF
Indubitably. Here is the Countess Merenburg, who has especially been looking forward to making your acquaintance. May I —

EDINE *approaches*
I'm vastly delighted. I beg you, Baron Neuhoff, not merely to introduce me to a man of such eminence, but ask that I be presented to him.

FAMOUS MAN *makes a bow*
I am most pleased, Countess.

EDINE
It would be carrying coals to Newcastle if I were to tell you that I belong to the most ardent readers of your renowned works. I am quite transported by such philosophical profundity, such immense erudition and such a lovely prose style.

FAMOUS MAN
You astound me, Countess. My works are not exactly light reading. They are not exclusively addressed to a public consisting of specialists, but they do presuppose a reader of more than common capacity to assimilate.

EDINE
Oh, by no means! Every woman ought to read such lovely, deep-reaching books so as to raise herself to a higher sphere. I keep saying this to Toinette Hechingen till I'm blue in the face.

FAMOUS MAN
Might I enquire which of my works has had the merit of arousing your attention?

EDINE
Naturally that wonderful work "On the Origin of all Religions". That has a depth, you know, and one draws such uplifting instruction out of it.

FAMOUS MAN *icily*
Hm. That is indeed a work much talked about.

EDINE
But not enough, by a long chalk. I was just saying to Toinette; that is something each one of us ought to have lying on the bedside-table.

FAMOUS MAN
The Press in particular has seen fit to mount an unfettered publicity campaign on behalf of this opus.

EDINE
How can you say such a thing! Such a work is just about the most grandiose —

FAMOUS MAN
I am most intrigued, Countess, to find you also among the eulogizers of this product. As for me, I have, as it happens, no knowledge of the book and should scarcely find it in me to wish to increase the readership of this confection.

EDINE
What? You are not the author?

FAMOUS MAN
The author of this journalistic compilation is my faculty colleague Brückner. There is indeed an unfortunate similarity in the name, but that is the only one.

EDINE
That shouldn't be allowed, that two famous philosophers have such similar names.

FAMOUS MAN
It is indeed regrettable, especially for me. Herr Brückner is, by the way, in no sense a philosopher. He is a philologist, I would say, a drawing-room philologist, or better still, a philological feature writer.

EDINE
I'm frightfully sorry to have produced this confusion. But I'm quite sure I have something from among your famous works at home, Professor. I read everything, you see, that's of any bit of benefit to one. At the moment I have at home a most interesting book on "Semipelagianism"and one about the "Soul of Radium". If you'd care to visit me in the Heugasse some time —

FAMOUS MAN *frostily*
It would be an honour for me, Countess. I have, of course a great many commitments.

EDINE *about to go, yet remaining standing*
But that's really such a shame that you're not the author! Now I can't put my question to you either! And I would have bet anything that you're the one and only person to answer it to my wholehearted satisfaction.

NEUHOFF
Won't you put your question to the Professor all the same?

EDINE
You are no doubt a man of more profound erudition than the other gentleman. *To* NEUHOFF Should I really? It matters tremendously for me to discover this. I would, for the life of me, love some reassurance.

FAMOUS MAN
Won't you take a seat, Countess?

EDINE *anxiously looking about her to see if no one is coming in; then rapidly:*
How do you imagine Nirvana to be?

FAMOUS MAN
Hm. In order to answer that question off the cuff, Herr Brückner would certainly be the right man to address. *A slight pause.*

EDINE
And now I must also return to my game of Bridge. Au revoir, Professor. *Exit.*

FAMOUS MAN *visibly disgruntled*
Hm. —

NEUHOFF
Poor dear Countess Edine! You musn't take offence on her account.

FAMOUS MAN *coldly*
It's not the first time that I have met with similar mix-ups among a lay public. I half suspect that that charlatan Brückner is purposely working towards such an end. You can scarcely guess at the distressing impression a grotesque and compromising situation, such as we have just experienced, leaves on my mind. To witness such paltry, half-baked knowledge, trumpeted abroad by a blackguard press, launched out on the broad tide of vulgarization — and to find oneself confounded with the very thing against which one had thought oneself unassailably armed with the icy silence of contempt —

NEUHOFF
But all this goes without saying, my esteemed Professor! I feel with you down to the subtlest nuance. To find oneself misunderstood in one's finest achievements from dawn to dusk — such is the sad fate —

FAMOUS MAN
In one's finest achievements.

NEUHOFF
To see just that nuance mistaken, which matters most —

FAMOUS MAN
The work of a lifetime set beside this journalistic —

NEUHOFF
Such is the sad fate of —

FAMOUS MAN
Put about by a blackguard press —

NEUHOFF
— of the uncommonly gifted man, when he plays into the hands of vulgar humanity, of women who cannot distinguish between a hollow mask and a man of true eminence.

FAMOUS MAN
To meet with the detested traces of mobocracy even in a salon —

NEUHOFF
Please don't upset yourself. How can a person of your rank — nothing an Edine von Merenburg and her like may voice, can even remotely approach you.

FAMOUS MAN

It is all the press, that witches' brew of every conceivable ingredient! But I had thought myself safe from all of that here. I see that I overestimated the exclusiveness of these circles, at least so far as the life of the mind is concerned.

NEUHOFF

Mind, and these people! Life — and these people! All those you meet with here don't in reality exist any more. They are all nothing but shadows. Nobody who moves about these drawing-rooms, belongs to the real world in which the century's intellectual crises are played out. Just look about you: a phenomenon such as that figure in the next room, from head to toe a balancing act in boundless self-confidence and trivialty, besieged by women and girls — Kari Bühl.

FAMOUS MAN

Is that Count Kari Bühl?

NEUHOFF

The man himself, the famous Kari.

FAMOUS MAN

I haven't yet had the opportunity of making his acquaintance. Are you and he friends?

NEUHOFF

Not the greatest, but sufficient for me to characterize him for you in a couple of words: a presumptuous, utter nonentity.

FAMOUS MAN

He enjoys exceptionally high rating among the best circles. He is reckoned quite a personality.

NEUHOFF

There's nothing about him that would withstand close scrutiny. In society I tolerate him partly out of habit; but you will have less than nothing to lose if you don't get to know him.

FAMOUS MAN *looks fixedly in that direction*

I should be most interested to make his acquaintance. Do you think I might lose face if I were to approach him?

NEUHOFF

You will be wasting your time with him, as with all these people here.

FAMOUS MAN

I should attach particular importance to being introduced to Count Bühl in a telling manner, perhaps through one of his close friends.

NEUHOFF

I would not wish to be counted among these, but I shall arrange things for you.

FAMOUS MAN

You are most obliging. Or do you think I might lose face, were I to approach him quite spontaneously?

NEUHOFF

You do the old boy too much honour either way if you take him that seriously.

FAMOUS MAN

I cannot deny that I attach particular weight to adding the subtle and stringent vote of the upper classes to those accolades my learning has already earned from a broad international lay public; in this I may be permitted to discern the afterglow of a none too common scholarly career. *Exeunt.*

SCENE THREE

ANTOINETTE *with* EDINE, NANNI *and* HUBERTA *have meanwhile appeared in the centre doorway and come forward.*

ANTOINETTE

Well, say something to me, give me some advice, when you can see how agitated I am. I shall do something irreparably stupid if no one stands by me.

EDINE

I vote we leave her alone. She must appear to run into him by accident,. If we go with her in convoy, then we really shall scare him off.

HUBERTA

He isn't one to get embarrassed. If he had wanted to speak to her alone, we just wouldn't exist for him.

ANTOINETTE

So let's just sit here together. Stay by me, all of you, but not too obviously.

They have sat down.

NANNI

We'll chat quite casually here: it mustn't by any means look as if you were chasing after him.

ANTOINETTE

If only I had the craftiness of that woman Helen; she runs after him wherever he goes and all the time it looks as if she were avoiding him.

EDINE
I'd be for leaving her to her own devices, and that Toinette should go up to him just as if nothing's the matter.

HUBERTA
Given the state's she's in, she can't be expected to go up to him just as if nothing's the matter.

ANTOINETTE *close to tears*
Don't keep telling me that I'm in a state! Help by diverting me somehow! Otherwise I shall lose all my composure. If only I had someone to flirt with here!

NANNI *about to get up*
I'll go and fetch Stani for her.

ANTOINETTE
Stani wouldn't help me *that* much. As soon as I know that Kari is somewhere in the same building, all the others don't matter to me any more.

HUBERTA
Perhaps Feri Uhlfeldt might still exist all the same.

ANTOINETTE
If Helen were in my position, she'd know what to do. She uses that Theophil Neuhoff for a screen, as bold as brass, and behind it she operates.

HUBERTA
But she never so much as looks at Theophhil, busy as she is pursuing Kari.

ANTOINETTE
Just say that to me once more if you want to see all the colour drain from my face. *Stands up.* Is he talking to her?

HUBERTA
Of course he's talking to her.

ANTOINETTE
All the time?

HUBERTA
As often as I've looked across.

ANTOINETTE
Oh my God, if you keep on telling me only unpleasant things, I shall start to look frightful! *She sits down once more.*

NANNI *about to get up*
If your friends are getting too much for you, then let us go. I'm also very fond of playing a hand.

ANTOINETTE
Oh do please stay, do give me some advice; tell me what I'm to do.

HUBERTA
If she sent her maid to his house an hour ago, she can't now start to act the offended party.

NANNI
On the contrary, I'd say. You must pretend that he means nothing to you. I know this from card games: if one takes up the cards casually, luck comes knocking. One always has to master that inner sense of superiority.

ANTOINETTE
At the moment I certainly feel superior, I must say!

HUBERTA
You're treating him in completely the wrong manner by just surrendering out of hand.

EDINE
If she'd only allow herself to be given guidance! I know all about men's characters.

ANTOINETTE
The most sensible thing for me to do is to go home.

NANNI:
Now who would want to throw in her hand so long as she still holds a few cards.

EDINE
If you'd only listen to some sound sense. I happen to have a real instinct for such psychological matters. It could definitely be arranged for your marriage to be annulled; it has, after all, stood all these years under moral coercion; and then, once annulled, Kari would marry you, if the thing were half-way properly wangled.

ANTOINETTE *with a start*
Is he coming? My God, how my knees are trembling.

HUBERTA
Crescence is coming. Pull yourself together.

ANTOINETTE *to herself*
Dear God, I simply can't stand her, nor she me; but I'll eat just about any humble pie since she's his sister.

SCENE FOUR

CRESCENCE *comes in from the right*
Good evening to you all; what are you up to then? Toinette looks rather the worse
for wear. Have you nothing to say for yourselves? So many young ladies too! Stani
should never have gone off to the club, should he?

ANTOINETTE *laboriously*
We are, for the time being, amusing ourselves very well without gentlemen.

CRESCENCE *without taking a seat*
What do you say to Helen; isn't she looking simply splendid tonight? She'll be so
alluring as a young wife that no one could possibly hold a candle to her.

HUBERTA
Has Helen suddenly come into favour with you, then?

CRESCENCE
You're all very sweet too. Toinette ought to take care of herself a bit more. She looks
as if she hasn't slept for three nights. *In going* I must go and tell Poldo Altennwyl
how brilliant I find Helen tonight. *Exit.*

SCENE FIVE

ANTOINETTE
Heavens, now I've as good as got it in writing that Kari wants to marry Helen.

EDINE
How come?

ANTOINETTE
Don't you notice how she's running around in circles for her future sister-in-law?

NANNI
Oh, go on with you, don't drive yourself to distraction for a mere trifle. He'll be
coming in at the door any minute now.

ANTOINETTE
If he comes in at such a moment, I shall be quite — *puts her little handkerchief to her
eyes* — devastated.

HUBERTA
Then let's go. Meanwhile she'll calm down.

ANTOINETTE
No, the two of you go and see if he's talking to Helen again; then you can interrupt him. You've interrupted me often enough, heaven knows, when I so much wanted to be alone with him. And Edine can stay with me.

They have all got to their feet, HUBERTA *and* NANNI *go out.*

SCENE SIX

ANTOINETTE *and* EDINE *sit down left, at the back.*

EDINE
My dear girl, you've handled this whole sorry business with Kari wrongly from the start.

ANTOINETTE
How would you know about that?

EDINE
I know this from Mademoiselle Feydeau, who told me everything down to the last detail, how you had already put the whole affair in jeopardy at Grünleiten.

ANTOINETTE
That malevolent gossip, what does she know about it!

EDINE
But how can she help it, if she heard you running barefoot down the stairs, and then saw you walking with him in the moonlight, your hair all loose. — You simply had far too down-to-earth an approach to the whole business from the start. Men are, of course, very down-to-earth, but for that reason something loftier must be introduced on our part. A man like Kari never met a woman in his life who might have injected a dash of idealism into him. And that's why he is himself quite incapable of injecting something loftier into a love affair, and this also applies vice versa. If only you'd asked for a wee bit of advice in the early stages, if only you'd allowed me to give you a bit of guidance, to recommend a few books — you'd be his wife today!

ANTOINETTE
Do go, Edine, I beg you; don't vex me.

SCENE SEVEN

HUBERTA *appears in the doorway*
Listen, Kari is coming. He's looking for you.

ANTOINETTE
Sweet Jesus! *They have all got up.*

NANNI *who has been looking out towards the right*
Helen is coming accross from the other drawing-room.

ANTOINETTE
Oh my God, just at the decisive moment, she has to come along and spoil everything for me. Well do something about it. Well, go towards her then. Just keep her away from that room!

HUBERTA
Do pull yourself together a little.

NANNI
We'll just move accross there quite inconspicuously.

SCENE EIGHT

HELEN *steps in from the right*
You all look as though you've been talking about me. *Silence.* Are you enjoying yourselves? Shall I send over some gentlemen for you?

ANTOINETTE *going over to her, almost without self-control*
We're having a fabulous time, and you're an angel, Darling, for looking after us so nicely. I haven't even said good evening to you yet. You're looking lovelier than ever. *Kisses her.* But do leave us on our own and go away.

HELEN
Am I in the way? Well, then I'll go again. *Exit.*

SCENE NINE

ANTOINETTE *strokes her cheek as though wishing to wipe away the kiss.*
What am I up to? Why do I let myself be kissed by her? By this viper, this false creature!

HUBERTA
Do pull yourself together just a little.

SCENE TEN

HANS KARL *has entered from the right*

ANTOINETTE *after a short interlude of silence, of cowering, goes up to him rapidly and steps quite close to him*
I've taken the letters and burnt them. I'm not the sentimental ninny my Agatha takes me for; as though I could cry my eyes out over some old letters. I simply have only

what I have at a given moment, and what I don't have, I try to forget. I don't live in the past; I'm not old enough for that.

HANS KARL
Shall we not sit down together? *Conducts her over to the armchairs.*

ANTOINETTE
I'm just not that clever: if one isn't artful, one hasn't got the strength to keep a hold on someone such as yourself. Because you belong to the same species as your nephew Stani. That I have to tell you, so as you'll know. I know you both. Monstrously selfish and lacking in feeling. *After a little pause* Well go on, say something!

HANS KARL
If you would allow me, I would like to remind you of a time —

ANTOINETTE
Ah, I won't let myself be maligned. — Not even by someone who was at one time not indifferent to me.

HANS KARL
At that time, I mean two years ago, you were temporarily estranged from your husband. You were in great danger of falling into the hands of a worthless man. Then someone came along — who happened by chance to be me. I wanted to — reassure you — that was my only thought — to draw you away from a threat — to which I knew you to be exposed — or at least sensed it as such. It was all a chain of accidents — an incompetence — I don't know what to call it —

ANTOINETTE
Those few days in Grünleiten are the only truly beautiful event of my entire life. I won't let them — I won't allow the memory to be slighted. *Stands up.*

HANS KARL *quietly*
It was all so lovely!

ANTOINETTE
"That happened by chance to be me." You wish to insult me with this. You've become cynical out there. A cynical man, that's the right expression. You've lost all your nuance for what is possible and what is impossible. How did you put it? It was an "incompetence" on your part. Why, you keep insulting me over and over again.

HANS KARL
A great deal was changed for me out there. But I did not become cynical. On the contrary, Antoinette. When I think back to our beginning, then it seems to me something so tender, so mysterious, that I hardly dare to call it back to mind. I have to ask myself: how did I ever reach the point? Was I really allowed? But then, *very quietly* I regret nothing.

ANTOINETTE *lowers her eyes*
All beginnings are beautiful.

HANS KARL
In every beginning lies eternity.

ANTOINETTE *without looking at him*
At bottom you consider everything possible and everything permissible. You don't wish to see how helpless is the creature you pass over — how vulnerable, for that might possibly arouse your conscience.

HANS KARL
I have none.

ANTOINETTE *looks at him.*

HANS KARL
Not in relation to us.

ANTOINETTE
I used to be one thing and then another in your eyes — and at this moment I so little know where I stand with you; it's as if there never existed anything between us at all. You are too dreadful.

HANS KARL
There's nothing wicked. The moment isn't wicked; merely the wish to hold fast is inadmissable. Only the act of clinging to what cannot be retained —

ANTOINETTE
Well, we don't live like the proverbial flies do, just from morning to night. We happen to be there the next day as well. That just doesn't suit you, or the likes of you.

HANS KARL
Everything that happens is brought about by chance. It is quite simply beyond us how accidental we all are, and how chance drives us towards one another and apart again; and how each one of us could live in unison with the other, if chance would have it so.

ANTOINETTE
I don't wish to —

HANS KARL *keeps talking without acknowledging her resistance*
Yet isn't it perfectly monstrous that Man had to find something in order to pull himself out of this morass by his own bootstraps. And so he discovered the institution which could create from the accidental and impure, what is necessary, permanent and valid: namely, marriage.

ANTOINETTE

I can sense that you're trying to hitch me up with my husband. There hasn't been an instant, since you've been sitting here, that you might have hoodwinked me without me noticing. You certainly do go the distance; you think you may do anything you like; first seduce and then insult into the bargain.

HANS KARL

I'm no seducer, Toinette, I'm not a woman-chaser.

ANTOINETTE

Yes, that's your little trick in getting round me, that you're no seducer, no ladies' man, that you're just a friend, but a true friend. You flirt with this just as you flirt with everything you possess and with everything you lack. If you had your way, one would not only need to be in love with you, but to love you to distraction, and then for your own sake and not just as a man — but rather — I no longer know how to put it; oh my God, why must the same man be so charming, and at the same time so monstrous and selfish and heartless!

HANS KARL

Do you know, Toinette, what the heart is; do you really know? When a man feels he has a heart for a woman, he can only show this in one way, by only one thing in the world: by permanence, by constancy. Only by that: that is the test, the only one there is.

ANTOINETTE

Stop going on about Ado — I cannot live with Ado.

HANS KARL

He loves you. Now and for ever. He chose you out of all the women in the world, and he has kept loving you and will continue to love you for ever. Do you know what that means? For ever, no matter what happens. To possess a friend who loves your whole being, for whom you are always quite beautiful, not just today and tomorrow but later, much later too; for whom the eyes are but a veil which passing years, or whatever else may come, cast over your face — in his eyes it doesn't exist, you are always what you are; the most beautiful, the beloved, the one and only woman.

ANTOINETTE

That's not how he chose me. He just married me. I know nothing about any of the rest of it.

HANS KARL:

But he knows about it.

ANTOINETTE

Everything you've been saying just isn't true. He's been talking himself into all this and he's talked you into it — you're all the same, you men, you and Ado and Stani, you're all cast in the same mould, and that's why you get along so well and can play each other's game so nicely.

HANS KARL
He hasn't talked me into it, that I know, Toinette. It's the sacred truth, and I know it — I must always have known it, but only out there did it become perfectly clear to me: there is something called chance, which apparently does with us what it will — yet amid all that chaos of being flung hither and thither, all that apathy and fear of death, we feel and we know: there is a necessity which chooses us from one moment to the next: it passes silently, quite close to the heart, yet with the cutting edge of a sword. Without it no more living would have been possible out there, but mere bestial blundering on. And the selfsame necessity also exists between men and women — and where it exists, there is the need to come together, for forgiveness and reconciliation and staying together. And then children may come along, and there's marriage and a sanctuary, despite everything —

ANTOINETTE *stands up*
Everything you've been saying amounts to nothing less than that you wish to get married; that you are soon going to marry Helen.

HANS KARL *remains seated, holds her back*
But I wasn't even thinking about Helen! I'm talking about you. I swear that I'm talking about you.

ANTOINETTE
But all your thoughts are revolving around Helen.

HANS KARL
I swear to you: I've got an assignment for Helen. A completely different one to what you're thinking. I'm going to tell her today —

ANTOINETTE
What are you going to tell her today — a secret?

HANS KARL
None that concerns me.

ANTOINETTE
But one that connects you with her?

HANS KARL
But no. Quite the contrary!

ANTOINETTE
The contrary? A goodbye — you're telling her what amounts to a goodbye between you and her?

HANS KARL
There's no need for a goodbye, since there never was anything between me and her. But if it gives you pleasure, Toinette, then it almost amounts to a goodbye.

ANTOINETTE
A goodbye for life?

HANS KARL
Yes, for life, Toinette.

ANTOINETTE *looks him full in the face*
For life? *Thoughtfully* Yes, she's a secretive one, and does nothing twice, and never says anything twice. She takes nothing back — she has herself firmly in hand: a single word must decide things for her. If you say to her: goodbye — then to her mind it is goodbye for ever. For her certainly. *After a little pause* I won't have you talking me into having Ado back. I don't like his hands. Nor his face. Nor his ears. *Very quietly* I love your hands though. — What exactly are you? Yes, who are you exactly? You're a cynic, a devil, that's what you are! To ditch me is too common for you. You're too heartless to keep me; too crafty to let me go. So you wish to be rid of me and still keep me in your power, and for that Ado is the very man for you — Go on and marry Helen. Marry whoever you like! I might perhaps know what to do with your amorous moods, but as for your bits of good advice, keep them. *About to leave.*

HANS KARL *takes a step towards her.*

ANTOINETTE
Leave me alone. *She takes a few steps, then half turning towards him* What's to become of me now? Just try talking me out of seeing Feri Uhlfeldt; he has such strength when he wants something. I told him I didn't like him; he said I couldn't tell what he's like as my friend, since I've not yet had him as a friend. Such words make one so confused. *Half through tears, tenderly* Now you're to blame for everything that happens to me.

HANS KARL
You do need one thing in this world: a friend. A true friend. *He kisses her hands* Please be good to Ado.

ANTOINETTE
I just can't be good to him.

HANS KARL
You can be, to anyone.

ANTOINETTE *gently*
Kari, don't you insult me, please.

HANS KARL
You must understand what I mean.

ANTOINETTE
I understand you well enough otherwise.

HANS KARL
Couldn't you just give it a try?

ANTOINETTE
For your sake alone, I could. But you'd have to be there to help me.

HANS KARL
Now you've given me half a promise.

SCENE ELEVEN

The FAMOUS MAN *has come in from the right: he attempts to approach* HANS KARL. *Neither of the two notice him.*

ANTOINETTE
You've promised me something.

HANS KARL
For the time being.

ANTOINETTE *close by him*
To love me a little!

FAMOUS MAN
Pardon me, I'm intruding. *Leaves quickly.*

HANS KARL *close by her*
But I do.

ANTOINETTE
Say something really sweet to me: just for the moment. The moment means everything. I can only live in the moment. I have such a poor memory.

HANS KARL
I am not in love with you, but I do love you a little.

ANTOINETTE
And what you're going to say to Helen will be a goodbye?

HANS KARL
A goodbye.

ANTOINETTE
Oh so that's how you're trading me in; that's how you're selling me off!

HANS KARL
But you were never closer to me.

ANTOINETTE
You will come to me often, to encourage me? You can persuade me of anything.
HANS KARL *kisses her on the forehead, almost unwittingly.*

ANTOINETTE
Thank you. *Runs off through the centre.*

HANS KARL *stands bemused, rouses himself*
Poor little Antoinette.

SCENE TWELVE

CRESCENCE *comes in through the centre, very rapidly*
Well, you certainly did that brilliantly. That's really first class, the way you wangle such a thing.

HANS KARL
What? But you can't possibly know.

CRESCENCE
What more do I need to know. I know it all. Antoinette has her eyes full of tears, she dashes past me; as soon a she realizes it's me, she throws her arms around my neck and is gone again like the wind. That tells me everything, doesn't it? You've had a serious word with her, you've addressed her better self, you've made clear to her that she need no longer pin her hopes on Stani, and you showed her the only way out of this tricky situation; that she ought to return to her husband and endeavour to lead a decent, quiet life.

HANS KARL
Yes, more or less. But it didn't work out like that in detail. I don't have your purposeful manner. I am easily deflected from my line of approach, that I have to admit.

CRESCENCE
But that's all beside the point. If you achieve so brilliant a result at such a pace; now, while you're in your stride, I can barely wait for you to conclude those two conversations with Helen and Poldo Altenwyl. I beg you, go to her, I'll keep my fingers crossed. Just remember, Stani's future happiness depends entirely on your powers of persuasion.

HANS KARL
Have no fear, Crescence, in talking with Antoinette Hechingen just now, I've found my principal lines of approach for my conversation with Helen. I'm quite in the right mood. You know, it's a weakness of mine that I so seldom see what's definite before me: but this time I do see it.

CRESCENCE
You see, that's the benefit of having a programme in mind. A certain coherence comes into the whole business. So let's go. We'll look for Helen together. She must be in one of the drawing-rooms, and when we've found her, I'll leave you alone with her. And as soon as we have a result, I'll dash to the telephone and have Stani come over at the double.

SCENE THIRTEEN

CRESCENCE *and* HANS KARL *go out left.* HELENE *with* NEUHOFF *come in from the right. One can hear subdued music being played from a remoter drawing-room.*

NEUHOFF *behind her*
Stay a moment. This worthless, empty, sickly music and this half light set you off marvellously.

HELEN *has stopped but then continues over towards the easy chairs to the left*
I don't enjoy acting as model, Baron Neuhoff.

NEUHOFF
Not even if I close my eyes?

HELEN *says nothing, stands to the left.*

NEUHOFF
Your very being, Helen! No one was ever quite as you are. Your simplicity is the product of an immense intensity. Motionless as a statue, you yet vibrate inwardly; no one even suspects it, but he who does, vibrates with you.

HELEN *looks at him, sits down.*

NEUHOFF *not so close*
Everything about you is wonderful. And yet, like all that is exalted, almost frighteningly commonplace.

HELEN
Is the exalted commonplace for you, then? That was a noble thought.

NEUHOFF
Perhaps one might become his wife — that was what your lips were about to say, Helen!

HELEN
Do you lip-read, as the deaf and dumb do?

NEUHOFF *a step closer*
You shall marry me, because you can sense my will in a world that knows no will.

HELEN *musing to herself*
Must one? Is it a dictate to which a woman must submit if she is chosen and desired?

NEUHOFF
There are aspirations which are worth little. These may be trodden upon by such lovely well-bred feet. Mine is worthy. It has led me halfway round the globe. Here it has found its goal. You have been found, Helen Altenwyl, by the strongest will on the farthest possible quest, here in the most feeble-willed of worlds.

HELEN
I belong to it and am not feeble-willed.

NEUHOFF
Your world has sacrificed everything to the lovely illusion, even strength. We who come from that nordic corner where the centuries pass us by, have retained our strength. Thus we stand on equal ground, and yet not quite on equal ground; and from this inequality springs my right over you.

HELEN
Your right?

NEUHOFF
The right of the strongest in mind over woman, whom he is capable of raising to the realm of the spiritual.

HELEN
I don't relish these mystical turns of phrase.

NEUHOFF
A touch of mysticism always prevails between two people who have recognized each other at first glance. This your pride should not deny.

HELEN *has stood up*
It denies it again and again.

NEUHOFF
Helen, in you I could find my salvation — my consummation, my self-fulfilment.

HELEN
I don't wish to know anyone who imposes such conditions on his life! *She takes a few paces past him: her eyes are fixed on the open door on the right where she entered.*

NEUHOFF
How your expression has changed! What is it, Helen?

HELEN *is silent, looks towards the right.*

NEUHOFF *has stepped behind her and follows her glance.*
Oh! Count Bühl has appeared on the screen. *He retreats from the door.* You sense his presence magnetically — but can't you see, you inscrutable being, that for him you don't even exist?

HELEN
I do exist for him, somehow I exist all right!

NEUHOFF
You're wasting your life! You lend him everything, even the strength with which he holds you.

HELEN
The strength with which a person holds one — that is surely given by God.

NEUHOFF
I'm amazed. What makes a Kari Bühl exert such fascination over you? Without deserts, even without effort, without will, without dignity —

HELEN
Without dignity!

NEUHOFF
That spineless, ambiguous person has no dignity.

HELEN
What sort of language is that you use?

NEUHOFF
My northern idiom possibly sounds a little sharp in your finely shaped ears. But I stand by its sharpness. I call a man ambiguous who half gives and half holds himself back — who holds back reserves in every direction — shows calculation in every direction —

HELEN
Calculation and Kari Bühl! Do you really see him so little for what he is! True, it's impossible to know his final word on anything, which in others is so easily known. That awkwardness which makes him so endearing, that timid pride, his condescension; all that is, of course, a game of hide-and-seek; it cannot, of course, be grasped by clumsy hands. — He is not hardened by vanity in the way that makes all others stiff and wooden — reason does not cheapen him, just as it makes something vulgar of most people — he is completely his own man — no one really knows him; small wonder, then, that you don't know him!

NEUHOFF
I have never seen you like this before, Helen. I'm enjoying this incomparable moment! For once I see you as God created you, body and soul. A spectacle for the gods. A plague on all softness in men and in women! But rigour which grows soft is magnificent beyond compare!

HELEN *is silent.*

NEUHOFF
You must allow me this; it is a sign of some superiority in a man if he is able to enjoy in a woman how she admires another. But I am able to do so, for I can belittle your admiration for Kari Bühl.

HELEN
You're confusing the nuances. You are piqued where it is out of place to be so.

NEUHOFF
I cannot be piqued by that which I simply disregard.

HELEN
You do not know him! You've hardly even spoken to him.

NEUHOFF
I paid him a visit —

HELEN *looks at him.*

NEUHOFF
It doesn't bear repeating how this man compromises you — you mean nothing to him. It is you he disregards.

HELEN *calmly*
No.

NEUHOFF
A duel was fought out between myself and him, a duel over you — and it was not I who was defeated.

HELEN
No, it was not a duel. It doesn't deserve so heroic a name. You went there to do just what I'm doing at this moment! *Laughs* I'm trying my best to see Count Bühl without letting him see me. But I do so without ulterior motives.

NEUHOFF
Helen!

HELEN
I have no thought of gaining anything which might serve my purpose!

NEUHOFF
You're treading me into the dust, Helen — and I'm letting you do so!

HELEN *is silent.*

NEUHOFF
And could nothing bring me closer?

HELEN
Nothing. *She takes a step towards the door on the right.*

NEUHOFF
Everything about you is lovely, Helen. When you sit down, it's as if you needed repose after some great heartache — and when you cross the room, it's as if you were moving towards some ultimate decision.

HANS KARL *has appeared in the doorway.*

HELEN *makes no reply to* NEUHOFF. *She walks slowly and silently over to the door on the right.*

NEUHOFF *quickly goes out to the left.*

SCENE FOURTEEN

HANS KARL
Yes, I need to talk to you.

HELEN
Is it something very serious?

HANS KARL
It does happen at times that things are required of one. Just about everything on earth comes about through talk. All the same, it's somewhat ridiculous to imagine that one can achieve some mind-boggling effect merely by a prudent choice of words, especially in a life where, what actually matters is that final, inexpressible nuance. All talk is based upon an unseemly surfeit of self-conceit.

HELEN
If everyone knew how unimportant they were, no one would open their mouth.

HANS KARL
You have such clear understanding, Helen. You always know so well, at any given moment, what actually matters.

HELEN
Do I?

HANS KARL
One can have such good rapport with you. One needs to watch one's step.

HELEN *looks at him*
One has to watch one's step?

HANS KARL

Indeed. Fellow-feeling is all very well, but to keep harping on it would be quite unseemly. For that reason one has to be especially on one's guard, if there is the sense that one has really good rapport.

HELEN

You have to do so, naturally. It's in your nature. Whoever might get the idea of pinning you down, would be the loser. But whoever believed that you had said your final farewell to her, might well find you saying how-d'you-do to her once more . — Antoinette had renewed charm for you today.

HANS KARL

You don't miss a thing!

HELEN

You rather use up these poor women in your own way, but you don't feel much affection for them at all. It means putting quite a brave face on it, or else lowering one's tone a bit, if one is to remain your lady friend.

HANS KARL

If you see me like that, I must actually be unlikeable in your eyes!

HELEN

Not in the least. You are charming. You are, for all that, like a child.

HANS KARL

Like a child? And yet I'm almost an old man. That's quite appalling. At thirty-nine, not to know where one stands in regard to oneself. Surely that's quite scandalous.

HELEN

I've never needed to reflect where I stand in regard to myself. In my case there's really nothing to consider; there's actually nothing but decent and considered behaviour.

HANS KARL

You have such a charming way with you!

HELEN

I don't wish to be sentimental; that just bores me. I wish to be down-to-earth, like anyone else, rather than sentimental. I don't wish to be eccentric either, nor do I wish to be flirtatious. So there's really nothing left for me to be, other than perfectly well-behaved.

HANS KARL *is silent.*

HELEN

Basically, we women can do whatever we like, sing scales if necessary, or spout politics, we always mean something different by it. — Singing scales lacks discretion, behaving well is discreeter; it expresses a particular intent not to commit an indiscretion, either in relation to oneself or to another.

HANS KARL
Everything about you is special and lovely. Nothing whatever could happen to you.
Go and marry whoever you choose, marry that Neuhoff; no, not Neuhoff if it can be
avoided, but the first full-blooded person that comes along, a person like my nephew
Stani. Yes indeed, Helen, marry Stani: he'd really love to, and anyhow, nothing
whatever can happen to you. You're quite indestructible, that may clearly be seen in
your face. I am always fascinated by a truly beautiful face — but yours —

HELEN
I wish you wouldn't talk to me like that, Count Bühl.

HANS KARL
But no, of course, beauty isn't the decisive thing about you, rather something entirely
different: within you lies the inevitable. You cannot understand me, of course; I
understand myself much less when I talk than when I'm silent. I can't even begin to
explain this to you; it's just something I had learnt to grasp out there: that there's
something written in people's faces. You see, even in a face such as Antoinette's, I
can read —

HELEN *with a fleeting smile*
Oh indeed, I'm quite sure of that.

HANS KARL *seriously*
Yes, it's a charming, sweet face, but there is always the same silent reproach engraved
upon it: why have all of you left me to that dreadful thing called chance? And this
gives her little mask something so helpless, despairing, that one might well fear for
her.

HELEN
But surely Antoinette is fully alive. She exists entirely for the moment, doesn't she?
Isn't that how women ought to be? The moment is everything. What does the world
want with a person like me? For me the moment simply doesn't exist: I stand here
and see the lamps alight over there and inside me I can already see them
extinguished. Here am I, speaking with you, we are quite alone in a room, but inside
me all this has already gone by: just as if someone of no significance had come in and
interrupted us, Huberta or Theophil Neuhoff or whoever; just as if all this had passed,
that I had sat with you here, hearing this music, which could hardly be less suited to
the two of us — then you are once again somewhere among the guests. And I too
am somewhere among the guests.

HANS KARL *quietly*
Any one who may share his life with you, must count himself lucky, and he should
thank God to the end of his days, Helen; to the end of his days, whoever he happens
to be. Don't take Neuhoff, Helen, — better take a man such as Stani, or rather not
Stani either; someone quite different; a good and noble person — and a proper man:
that is, everything I'm not. *He stands up.*

HELEN *also stands up, sensing that he is about to go*
But you're saying goodbye to me!

HANS KARL *doesn't answer.*

HELEN
That too I knew in advance: that the moment would come when when you would quite suddenly say goodbye to me and make an end — where there never was anything. As for those who actually were involved with you, to them you can never say goodbye.

HANS KARL
Helen, there are certain reasons.

HELEN
I believe I have had thoughts about every conceivable thing concerning the two of us at some time past. This is how we stood at some moment, this is how insipid music was playing, and this is how you said goodbye to me, once and for all.

HANS KARL
It isn't just the outcome of a moment, Helen, that I'm saying goodbye to you. Oh no, you musn't believe that. For if one has to say goodbye to someone, there's surely something behind it all.

HELEN
What then?

HANS KARL
Then one must very much belong to someone, and still not be permitted wholly to belong.

HELEN
What do you mean by that?

HANS KARL
Out there one sometimes had a feeling that — but my God, who could possibly describe all that!

HELEN
Yes, to me, now.

HANS KARL
There were certain hours, towards evening or at night, the early dawn with the morning star — Helen, you were then very close by me. Then there was the time we were buried alive, you've heard about that —

HELEN
Yes, I did hear about it —

HANS KARL

It was merely a moment, thirty seconds they said, but inwardly it has another dimension. For me it was a whole lifetime that I lived through, and during that part of a life you were my wife. Isn't that funny?

HELEN

I was your wife?

HANS KARL

Not my future wife. That's the strange thing. Quite simply, my wife. As a *fait accompli*. The whole thing had something of the past about it rather than of the future.

HELEN *is silent.*

HANS KARL

My God, I'm just impossible, as I keep telling Crescence! Here am I sitting next to you at a soiree and getting lost in story-telling like old Millesimo, God rest his soul, who in the end people left sitting there with his pointless anecdotes; but he never took any notice and kept telling his stories all on his own.

HELEN

But I'm not going to leave you sitting there; I'm listening, Count Kari. You wanted to tell me something; what was it?

HANS KARL

Well then: it was a very subtle lesson taught me there by a higher power. I shall tell you, Helen, what that lesson meant.

HELEN *has sat down, he also sits down, the music has stopped.*

HANS KARL

Clearly I was supposed to have impressed upon me at a given moment, what happiness might have been like, had I not gambled it away. By what means I gambled it away, you know as well as I do.

HELEN

I know as well as you do?

HANS KARL

By not having recognized, whilst I still had the time, where the one and only thing that really mattered might lie. That I had failed to register this, happened to be a weakness of character in me. And so I did not pass this test. Later, in the field hospital, during many a calm day and night, I was able to register all this with an uncanny clarity and lucidity.

HELEN

Was it this that you wished to tell me, purely this?

HANS KARL

Convalescence is such a strange condition. During that time the whole world was restored to me as something pure, something new and yet so self-evident. I was then suddenly able to perceive what this means: a human being, and what this must be like: two human beings who put their lives together and become as *one* person. I was able to imagine — at least in surmise — what it really means, how sacred a thing it is, and how marvellous. And the strange thing is, that it wasn't my marriage which was, quite unconsciously, at the centre of these thoughts — though it's quite conceivable that I might still marry — but it was your marriage.

HELEN

My marriage! My marriage — to whom then?

HANS KARL

I can't say: but I was able to imagine it all in very clear terms, how everything was to be, how it would take place, with very few people attending, all very sacred and solemn; and how it would all be as befits your eyes and your brow and those lips of yours, which can say nothing superfluous, and your hands, which could never seal anything unworthy — and I even heard you say 'Yes', pronounced very clearly and purely by your clear, pure voice — from quite a distance, since of course I wasn't actually present; obviously I wasn't present! — How should I, as an outsider, be there at that ceremony. — But I'm very glad to have let you know where I stand with you. — And that can, naturally, be done only at a privileged moment, like the present, as it were, at a definitive moment —

HELEN *is close to swooning, but controls herself.*

HANS KARL *with tears in his eyes*

Oh Lord, now I've completely upset you; it's all because of my impossible behaviour; I get emotional at once if I speak or hear of anything that isn't utterly banal — it's all to do with my nerves since that business; but it obviously affects sensitive people such as you — I just don't belong in company — I keep saying so to Crescence — I do beg your pardon a thousand times; please forget all this, whatever confused nonsense I kept ranting on about — at such farewell occasions, a thousand memories tend to become confused — *hastily, since he senses that they are no longer alone —* but if you've got yourself in hand, obviously you avoid airing them in public — goodbye, Helen, goodbye.

FAMOUS MAN *has entered from the right.*

HELEN *scarcely in control of herself*
Goodbye! *Each wishes to take the other's hand, yet neither hand finds the other.*

HANS KARL *tries to exit left.*

FAMOUS MAN *steps up to him.*

HANS KARL *looks round to the left.*

CRESCENCE *enters from the left.*

FAMOUS MAN
It has long been my eager wish, your Lordship —

HANS KARL *hurries off to the right*
Do excuse me, Sir! *Pushes past him.*

CRESCENCE *steps towards Helen, who stands there pale as death —*

FAMOUS MAN *has left in embarrassment.*

HANS KARL *reappears in the doorway to the right, looks in as though undecided and disappears again immediately when he sees* CRESCENCE *with* HELEN.

HELEN *to* CRESCENCE, *almost in a swoon*
Is it you, Crescence? He came back in once more, didn't he? Did he say anything else? *She reels,* CRESCENCE *holds her.*

CRESCENCE
Oh but I'm so happy. Your being so deeply moved, makes me so happy!

HELEN
Forgive me, Crescence, don't take it amiss! *Breaks away and runs off left.*

CRESCENCE
The two of you are much more in love than you know, Stani and you! *Wipes her eyes.*

The curtain falls.

ACT THREE

Vestibule in the Altenwyls' house. To the right an exit to the driveway. Stairs centre stage leading up to a gallery from which two double doors, one right and one left, lead to the actual interior rooms. Below, next to the staircase, low divans or bench seats.

SCENE ONE

VALET *stands beside the exit to the right. Other servants, standing outside, are visible through the glass panes of the porch. The valet calls out to the other servants*
Court Counsellor Professor Brücke!

The FAMOUS MAN *comes down the stairs. A servant comes from the right with a fur coat inside which there hang a couple of mufflers, together with overshoes.*

VALET *whilst helping the* FAMOUS MAN *into his coat*
Does the Court Counsellor wish to call a cab?

FAMOUS MAN
No thanks. Did his Lordship Count Bühl not leave ahead of me just now?

VALET
Just this very moment.

FAMOUS MAN
Did he leave by car?

VALET
No, his Lordship sent his car away; he saw two gentlemen drive up in front, stepped behind the porter's lodge and let them pass. He will only just have left the building.

FAMOUS MAN *hurrying along*
I'll catch him up. *He leaves, and at the same time* STANI *and* HECHINGEN *are to be seen entering.*

SCENE TWO

STANI *and* HECHINGEN *enter, a servant behind each of them, who takes their overcoat and hat.*

STANI *with a sign of greeting to the* FAMOUS MAN *as he passes*
Good evening, Wenzel; my mother is here, is she?

VALET
Yes Sir, her Ladyship is at the card table. *Exit as do the other servants.*

STANI *intending to go up.*

HECHINGEN *stands to one side by a mirror, visibly nervous. Another of the* ALTENWYL *servants comes down the stairs.*

STANI *stops the servant*
You know me, don't you?

SERVANT
Yes indeed, Sir.

STANI
Go through the drawing-rooms for me and look for Count Bühl until you find him. Then go up to him without ceremony and say I'd like a quick word with him, either in the corner room of the picture gallery or in the Chinese smoking room. Understood? So what will you say?

SERVANT
I shall say that Count Freudenberg wishes to have a word in private with his Lordship, either in the corner room —

STANI
Fine.

Exit SERVANT.

HECHINGEN
Pst, you, servant*!*

SERVANT *does not hear him, goes in upstairs.*

STANI *has sat down.*

HECHINGEN *looks at him.*

STANI
If you could just go in without me, I'd appreciate it. I've sent a message upstairs and I'll wait here a moment until he brings me the answer.

HECHINGEN
I'll keep you company.

STANI
No, I beg you not to be detained by me. You were in such a hurry to get here —

HECHINGEN
My dear Stani, you see me here in a very peculiar situation. Once I step accross the threshold of this drawing-room, my future destiny will be decided.

STANI *irritated by* HECHINGEN*'s nervous pacing up and down*
Wouldn't you care to sit down? As I said, I'm only waiting for the servant.

HECHINGEN
I can't sit down, I'm too agitated.

STANI
You knocked back the bubbly a bit too fast, I shouldn't wonder.

HECHINGEN
At the risk of boring you to death, my dear Stani, I have to confess to you that something of vast importance is at stake for me at this very hour.

STANI *while* HECHINGEN *moves away again, nervous and distracted*
But there's very often something or other serious at stake. What matters is not letting anyone notice.

HECHINGEN *closer once more*
Your Uncle Kari has, out of the goodness of his heart, taken it upon himself to have a word with Antoinette, with my wife, the outcome of which, as I say —

STANI
My Uncle Kari?

HECHINGEN
I told myself that my destiny could hardly be placed in the hands of a nobler, or a more selfless friend —

STANI
But of course — If only he can have found the time —

HECHINGEN
What's that?

STANI
He sometimes takes on rather too much, does Uncle Kari. Whenever anyone at all wants something of him — he just can't say no.

HECHINGEN
It was agreed that I should wait at the club for a signal by telephone, whether I should come over here or whether my appearance is not yet opportune.

STANI
Ah. Then in your place I should most definitely have waited.

HECHINGEN
It was simply more than I could bear to wait any longer. Just consider what is at stake for me!

STANI

One just has to rise that little bit above all such decisions. Aha! *Sees the servant who has stepped out above.*

SERVANT *comes down the stairs.*

STANI *goes towards him, leaves* HECHINGEN *standing.*

SERVANT

No, I believe his Lordship must have left.

STANI

You believe? I told you, you must look around until you find him.

SERVANT

Various guests have also been asking; his Lordship must have disappeared quite unnoticed.

STANI

Confound it! Then go to my mother and give her the message that I ask her most urgently to come out to me for a moment into the outer drawing-room. I must speak to my uncle or to her before I go in.

SERVANT

Very well. *Goes upstairs again.*

HECHINGEN

My instinct tells me that Kari will step out any minute now to announce the outcome to me, and that it is to be a happy one.

STANI

You possess that secure an instinct? My congratulations.

HECHINGEN

Something stopped him telephoning, but he wanted to call me over. I feel I'm in unbroken contact with him.

STANI

Fantastic!

HECHINGEN

It's mutual with us. Very often he says something aloud that I had just been thinking to myself at that moment.

STANI

You're obviously a superb medium.

HECHINGEN

My dear friend, when I was a young pup such as yourself, I wouldn't have thought many a thing possible, but when you've put your first thirty-five years behind you, a whole lot of things begin to dawn on you. It's just as though one had previously been deaf and blind.

STANI
You don't say!

HECHINGEN
You know, I actually owe Kari a further stage in my education. I think it important to make clear, that without him I should simply never have found my way out of my muddled situation in life.

STANI
Now that's something.

HECHINGEN
A special being like Antoinette, for all that I chanced to be her husband, this means nothing whatsoever; one simply hasn't an inkling about such inner refinemment. I would have it known that such a being is a butterfly whose pollen should be treated with utmost care. If you only knew her, I mean more closely —

STANI *makes a well-meaning gesture.*

HECHINGEN
Now I consider my relationship to her like this; that it is quite simply my obligation to allow her that freedom which her erratic, fanciful nature demands. She is by nature a *grande dame* of the eighteenth century. Only by granting her full freedom can one bind her to oneself.

STANI
Ah.

HECHINGEN
One needs to be magnanimous, that's what I have to thank Kari for. I should by no means find anything irremediable in liberally fostering close relations with any man who admires her.

STANI
I understand.

HECHINGEN
I would endeavour to befriend him, not from any design, but quite unreservedly. I would want to be generous and obliging: that's the way Kari showed me to take people; with a light, flexible touch.

STANI
But one need not take everything Uncle Kari says quite so literally.

HECHINGEN
Not quite literally, of course. But pray don't overlook the fact that I have a precise feel for what's needed. It all comes down to a certain *je ne sais quoi*, a certain gracefulness — I mean to say, it must all be an ongoing impromptu. *He paces nervously up and down.*

STANI
One must above all know how to keep up appearances. For example, if Uncle Kari were to await a decision on whatever matter, not a soul could tell by looking at him.

HECHINGEN
But of course. He would stand behind that statue or that large azalea over there and banter away with the greatest nonchalance — I can just picture it to myself! At the risk of boring you to death, I swear that I could feel with him every little nuance that would pass through his mind.

STANI
However, since we cannot both stand behind the azalea, and that idiot of a servant is just not coming back, we should perhaps go up.

HECHINGEN
Yes, let's both go. It does me good not having to live through this moment on my own. My dear Stani, I feel such a sincere liking for you! *Puts his arm through* STANI's.

STANI *whilst removing his arm from* HECHINGEN's
But perhaps not arm in arm like two countesses on their very first outing, but each man for himself.

HECHINGEN
Oh but of course, just as you please.

STANI
I would suggest that you start off first. I shall then follow at once.

HECHINGEN *goes ahead and disappears upstairs.*

STANI *follows him.*

SCENE THREE

HELEN *steps out through a small hidden door in the left-side wall. She waits until* STANI *is no longer visible above. She then calls quietly over to the* VALET
Wenzel, Wenzel, I have something to ask you.

VALET *goes quickly over to her*
At your service, your Ladyship.

HELEN *with lightness of tone*
Did you notice whether Count Bühl has left?

VALET
Indeed his Lordship did leave, five minutes ago.

HELEN
He left nothing?

VALET
How does your Ladyship mean?

HELEN
A letter or a message to pass on.

VALET
Not with me. I shall ask the other servants at once. *Goes across.*

HELEN *stands and waits.*

STANI *is seen above. He tries to see who* HELEN *is speaking to, and disappears again.*

VALET *returns to* HELEN
No, nothing at all. He sent his car away, lit a cigar and left.

HELEN *says nothing.*

VALET *after a short pause*
Will there be anything else, your Ladyship?

HELEN
Yes, Wenzel, I shall come back in a few minutes, and then I shall be going out.

VALET
Going out by car, now, this evening?

HELEN
No, walking, on foot.

VALET
Has someone been taken ill?

HELEN
No, no one is ill. I have to speak to someone.

VALET
Does your Ladyship wish for someone to accompany her, apart from the English
Miss?

HELEN
No, I shall go by myself, not even Miss Jekyll need accompany me. I'll leave at a moment when none of the guests is leaving. And I shall give you a letter for my father.

VALET
Does your Ladyship then wish me to take it in straight away?

HELEN
No, give it to Papa once he has seen off the last guests.

VALET
When all the guests have taken their leave?

HELEN
Yes, the moment he asks for the lights to be put out. But then you should stay with him. I want you to — *she hesitates.*

VALET
Yes, your Ladyship?

HELEN
How old was I, Wenzel, when you first came into our household?

VALET
You were just a five-year old girl, your Ladyship.

HELEN
Thank you, Wenzel, that will be all. I shall come out here, and you'll give me a sign to say that the way is clear. *Stretches out her hand to be kissed.*

VALET
At your service. *Kisses her hand.*

HELEN *goes out again through the small door.*

SCENE FOUR

ANTOINETTE *and* NEUHOFF *come from the stairs to right-hand side out of the conservatory.*

ANTOINETTE
That was Helen. Was she alone? Did she see me?

NEUHOFF
I believe not. But who cares? At any rate you need not fear that look.

ANTOINETTE
I'm afraid of her. Whenever I think of her, I get the feeling that someone has lied to me. Let's go somewhere else; we can't sit here in the vestibule.

NEUHOFF
Set your mind at rest. Karl Bühl has gone. I just saw him as he was leaving.

ANTOINETTE
Just this very minute?

NEUHOFF *understands what she is thinking of*
He left unnoticed and was unaccompanied.

ANTOINETTE
What?

NEUHOFF
A certain person did not accompany him here and has not spoken to him for the last half hour that he was here. I was able to find this out: rest assured.

ANTOINETTE
He swore to me that he would say goodbye to her for ever. I have to see her face; then I'd know for sure —

NEUHOFF
That face is hard as stone. Stay here with me.

ANTOINETTE
I —

NEUHOFF
Your face is enchanting. Other faces hide everything. Yours is one continual confession. One could wrest from this face everything that ever passed through your mind.

ANTOINETTE
One could? Possibly — if one had the slightest right to do such a thing.

NEUHOFF
One claims that right as it arises from the moment. You are a woman; a real and enchanting woman. You belong to no one and to everyone! No: you have never yet belonged to anyone; you are still waiting.

ANTOINETTE *with a little nervous laugh*
Not for you!

NEUHOFF
Yes, precisely for me; I mean, for the man you do not yet know, for the real man, for chivalry, for kindliness which is rooted in strength. Because the Karis of this world

have only mistreated you, deceived you from first to last; that sort of person is without kindliness, without a core, without backbone, without loyalty! These parasites, to which a being like you falls prey again and again; unrewarded, unthanked, unblest, humiliated in her tenderest womanhood. *Tries to capture her hand.*

ANTOINETTE
How heated you've become! But I'm quite safe from you; your cold, calculating reason rears its ugly head out of every word you say.

NEUHOFF
My reason, how I hate it! I wish to be free of it, I have no other desire than to lose it with you, my sweet little Antoinette. *He attempts to take her hand.*

HECHINGEN *is seen above, but steps back again immediately.*

NEUHOFF *has seen him, does not take her hand, changes his posture and the expression on his face.*

ANTOINETTE
Ah, now I've seen right through you! How quickly all this can change in your face! I'll tell you what just happened: just now Helen passed by upstairs, and in that instant I was able to read you like an open book. Spite and impotence, anger, shame, and the desire to get me — *faute de mieux* — all this was there at the same time. Edine bullies me for not reading complicated books. But all that was quite complicated and yet I managed to read it in a flash. Don't try too hard on my account. I'm not interested.

NEUHOFF *bends over towards her*
You shall so desire!

ANTOINETTE *stands up*
Oho! I'm not interested! Not interested, do you hear! For whatever it is that's trying to escape your eyes and wants me in its power, but merely wants! — even if it is something very manly — still, I don't like it. And if that's the best part of you, then each one of us women, even the commonest, has something inside her that's better than your very best, and is inured against your very best by that little bit of fear. Yet not the sort of fear that makes one giddy, but one that is quite sober, quite prosaic. *She walks towards the staircase and remains standing once more.* Do you follow me? Do I make myself plain? I am afraid of you, but not enough, and that's your hard luck. Goodbye, Baron Neuhoff. NEUHOFF *has left quickly by way of the conservatory.*

SCENE FIVE

HECHINGEN *steps in above, he comes down the stairs very quickly.*

ANTOINETTE *is dismayed and steps back.*

HECHINGEN
Toinette!

ANTOINETTE
And now this!

HECHINGEN
What's that you say?

ANTOINETTE
I'm taken by surprise — surely you must see that.

HECHINGEN
And I'm a happy man. I thank the good Lord, I thank my good fortune, I thank this moment!

ANTOINETTE
You look altered somehow. Your expression is different. I'm not sure what the reason might be. Are you not quite yourself?

HECHINGEN
Is it not perhaps because these black eyes have not looked at me for so long?

ANTOINETTE
Surely it isn't that long ago since we last saw each other.

HECHINGEN
To see and to look are two different things, Toinette. *He has come closer to her.*

ANTOINETTE *draws back.*

HECHINGEN
Perhaps it is something else, though, that has changed me, If I may be so immodest as to speak about myself.

ANTOINETTE
What then? Have you become interested in someone?

HECHINGEN
To see your charm, your pride at play, to see the entire woman one loves suddenly there before one; to see her live!

ANTOINETTE
Ah, so it's all about me.

HECHINGEN
Yes, about you. I was so happy to see you for once just as you are; and for once I had not inhibited you. Oh, what my thoughts were, as I stood up there! This woman, desired by all and refusing all! My destiny, your destiny, for it belongs to both of us. Sit down here at my side! *He has sat down, stretches out a hand towards her.*

ANTOINETTE
We can talk together just as well standing up, since we're such old acquaintances.

HECHINGEN *has got up again*
I have never yet known you. I needed first to have new eyes. The man who comes to you here is a different man, a changed person.

ANTOINETTE
You have such a new tone to your speech. Where did you manage to acquire that?

HECHINGEN
The man speaking to you here is someone you do not know, Toinette, just as he has not known you! And one who has no other wish, who dreams of nothing else, other than knowing you and being known by you.

ANTOINETTE
Ado, I beg you please, don't speak to me as though I were some dining-car acquaintance straight off an express train.

HECHINGEN
One I so wish to travel with, travel to the ends of the earth! *Tries to kiss her hand; she withdraws it.*

ANTOINETTE
I beg you, can't you see that this is getting on my nerves. An elderly married couple must surely preserve a certain tone. One doesn't change that, does one; it's quite enough to make one giddy.

HECHINGEN
I know nothing of an elderly married couple: I know nothing of our situation.

ANTOINETTE
But that happens to be the given situation.

HECHINGEN
Given? All that doesn't exist at all. There's just you and me, and everything starts again afresh.

ANTOINETTE
Oh no, there's no starting again afresh.

HECHINGEN
The whole of life is a constant new beginning.

ANTOINETTE

No, no, I beg you please, stick to your old groove. Otherwise I simply can't endure it. Don't be annoyed with me; I have a little migraine. I had actually wanted to drive home earlier, before I knew that you'd — how was I to know!

HECHINGEN

You were not to know what kind of man it would be that stands before you; that he's not your husband but a new, impassioned admirer, no less enflamed than a twenty-year-old youngster! That's what confuses you and makes you reel. *Tries to take her hand.*

ANTOINETTE

No, it doesn't make me reel, it completely sobers me up. It brings me so far down to earth that it makes everything seem wretched, as I do to myself. I've just had an unlucky night. Please do me one small favour and let me go home.

HECHINGEN

Oh, Antoinette!

ANTOINETTE

I mean if you had wished to say something specific to me, then do so; I'll gladly listen to it, but one thing I ask of you! Do say it in your usual tone, just as always.

HECHINGEN *dejected and sobered down, is silent.*

ANTOINETTE

Well say it: say what you wanted to say to me.

HECHINGEN

I'm upset to find that my presence seems on the one hand to astonish you, on the other to be burdensome. I had indulged the hope that a certain dear friend might have seized the opportunity of addressing you on my behalf about my unchanging feelings towards you. I had half assumed, on that basis, that a spontaneous exchange between us might possibly reveal, or at any rate bring about, a renewed situation. — I would ask you not to overlook the fact that you have not, to date, afforded me the opportunity of speaking to you of my inner feelings — I view my relationship to you, Antoinette, in this light — am I boring you greatly?

ANTOINETTE

Oh, please, do go on. You had wanted to say something to me, hadn't you? Otherwise I simply can't explain your coming here.

HECHINGEN

I view our relationship as one which binds me, only me, Antoinette; which places me , only me, under a term of probation whose duration you alone may determine.

ANTOINETTE

But what's the purpose of this, where is this going to lead?

HECHINGEN
If I am to consult my own inner feelings, Toinette —

ANTOINETTE
Yes, what if you do consult in that way? *She clutches her forehead.*

HECHINGEN
— then, of course, it needs no lengthy scrutiny. I shall ever and again endeavour to adopt your standpoint in face of the world, shall always be the champion of your charm and your freedom. And if challenged by deliberate distortions from any quarter, I shall triumphantly point to what took place here but a few minutes hence, as eloquent proof of how equal you are to putting in their place such men as desire and impose on you.

ANTOINETTE *nervously*
What exactly?

HECHINGEN
You are much desired. Your type is that of the eighteenth-century *grande dame.* I quite fail to see anything reprehensible in that. Not the fact, but the nuance is to be respected. I am most keen to establish that, whatever your conduct, your *intentions* are for me above any hint of suspicion.

ANTOINETTE *close to tears*
My dear Ado, you really mean well, but my migraine increases with every word you speak.

HECHINGEN
Oh; I'm so sorry. All the more so, since these moments are infinitely precious to me.

ANTOINETTE
Please be so good — *she reels.*

HECHINGEN
I understand. A car?

ANTOINETTE
Yes. Edine permitted me to take hers.

HECHINGEN
At once. *Goes and gives orders. Returns with her coat. Helping her on with it*
Is that all I can do for you?

ANTOINETTE
Yes, that's all.

VALET *by the glass door, announces*
The car for her Ladyship, the Countess.

ANTOINETTE *leaves very quickly.*

HECHINGEN *is about to follow her but holds back.*

SCENE SIX

STANI *from behind, out of the conservatory. He appears to be looking for someone*
Ah, it's you. Have you by any chance seen my mother?

HECHINGEN
No. I wasn't in the drawing-rooms. I've just taken my wife to her car. It was a situation that defies belief.

STANI *preoccupied with his own affair*
I just don't understand. Mama first asks me to come to the conservatory, then she sends a message asking me to wait here on the stairs —

HECHINGEN
I really must have a proper chat with Kari now.

STANI
Then you'll have to leave and look for him.

HECHINGEN
My instinct tells me, he has only left so as to look for me at the club and that he'll be coming back. *Goes upstairs.*

STANI
Well, if one possesses that kind of an instinct, one that tells one everything! Ah! There's Mama!

SCENE SEVEN

CRESCENCE *comes out below left, alongside the staircase*
Here I am coming up the servants' stairs; these servants cause nothing but mis-understanding. First he tells me that you asked me to come to the conservatory, then he says the gallery —

STANI
Mama, this is an evening where one simply can't escape confusion of every kind. If it weren't for you, I was actually on the point of driving home on the spot, taking a shower and going to bed. I can take a good deal, but to be put in an awkward position, that, to me, is something quite odious; that really taxes my nerves to the full. Now I must urge you to bring me up to date.

CRESCENCE

Well, I simply cannot understand that your Uncle Kari could have left without giving me so much as a hint. That is just one of his many distracted habits. I'm quite beside myself, my dear boy.

STANI

Be so good as to explain the situation a little. Be so good as to tell me in broad outline, at least, what has happened.

CRESCENCE

But everything went exactly according to plan. First of all, your Uncle Kari and Antoinette had a most agitated conversation together —

STANI

That was the first mistake. I knew that in advance; that was all too complicated a matter. Please do continue!

CRESCENCE

What more do you expect me to say? Antoinette rushes past me, completely beside herself, immediately after, Uncle Kari sits down next to Helen —

STANI

It's just too complicated to conduct two such conversations successfully in one evening. And Uncle Kari —

CRESCENCE

The chat with Helen goes on forever, I come to the door — Helen falls into my arms, I'm overjoyed, she runs off all bashful, as is only right, I rush to the telephone and summon you over here!

STANI

Well I ask you, I know all that; but please enlighten me as to what the deuce actually took place here!

CRESCENCE

I fly breathless through the rooms looking for Kari; don't find him. I then have to return to the card game; you can imagine how I played. Mariette Stradonitz opens the bidding with hearts, I reply with diamonds, constantly praying to all fourteen Holy Helpers. Immediately after, I revoke with spades. Finally I'm able to get up; I look around for Kari; I can't find him! I go through all the pitch dark rooms right up to Helen's door. I hear her weeping inside. I knock and say my name: she doesn't answer. I slip back down to the card game. Mariette asks me three times if I'm feeling ill. Louis Castaldo looks at me as if I were a ghost. —

STANI

I understand everything.

CRESCENCE
How come? I don't understand a thing.

STANI
Everything, everything. The whole thing's clear to me now.

CRESCENCE
So tell me; how do you see it then?

STANI
Clear as daylight. Antoinette has, in her despair, created some gossip; she deduced from her chat with Uncle Kari that I'm lost to her for good. A woman who is in despair totally loses all composure; she then goes slinking up to Helen and made such an almighty fuss that Helen, in her pride and her gargantuan touchiness, decided to renounce me, even if it were to break her heart.

CRESCENCE
And that's why she didn't open the door for me.

STANI
And Uncle Kari, when he realized what damage he had done, made himself scarce at once.

CRESCENCE
Oh but then things do seem to look pretty bad after all! Yes, my dear young lad, what have you to say now?

STANI
My dear Mama, then all I have to say is this; and it's the only thing a man of quality can say to himself in any awkward situation: one remains what one is, and no bit of good or bad luck can alter that by one jot.

CRESCENCE
You're a dear sweet boy, and I adore you for your bearing; but that's not a reason for throwing in the towel!

STANI
I do beg you to spare me any awkward position.

CRESCENCE
For a person with your fine demeanour there can be no awkward position. I'll look for Helen now and I'll ask her what happened between now and a quarter to ten.

STANI
I earnestly implore you —

CRESCENCE
But my dear boy, you're far too precious to me, for me to want to force you on any family, were it even that of the Emperor of China. But on the other hand, Helen is

also too dear to me, for me to wish to sacrifice her happiness to that gossip of a jealous goose, Antoinette. So do me the favour by staying here and taking me home afterwards. Surely you can see how agitated I am. *She goes up the stairs* STANI *follows her.*

SCENE EIGHT

HELEN *has come through the hidden door on the left, dressed in a coat, as if to go out. She hesitates until* CRESCENCE *and* STANI *can no longer see her. Simultaneously,* HANS KARL *can be glimpsed through the glass door to the right; he puts down his hat, stick, and overcoat, and appears.* HELEN *has seen* HANS KARL *before he catches sight of her. Her expression changes completely in an instant. She lets her coat fall from her shoulders, and it remains lying behind the stairs, then she steps up towards* HANS KARL.

HANS KARL *disconcerted*
Helen, you're still here?

HELEN *here, and from now on, maintaining a completely firm, decisive manner, and in a light, almost aloof tone*
Yes, this is my home.

HANS KARL
You appear different from usual. Something has happened!

HELEN
Yes, something has happened.

HANS KARL
When? Quite suddenly?

HELEN
An hour ago, I believe.

HANS KARL *uncertain*
Something disagreeable?

HELEN
What?

HANS KARL
Something upsetting?

HELEN
Oh, yes indeed.

HANS KARL
Something irreparable?

HELEN

That remains to be seen. Look, do you see what's lying over there?

HANS KARL

Over there? A fur coat. A lady's coat it seems.

HELEN

Yes, my coat is lying there. I had wanted to go out.

HANS KARL

Go out?

HELEN

Yes, and I'll let you know my reason too. But first you will tell me why you've returned. That's not really usual behaviour.

HANS KARL *hesitating*

It always embarrasses me a little if I'm asked quite so directly.

HELEN

Yes, I'm asking you directly.

HANS KARL

I can't easily explain it.

HELEN

We could sit down. *They sit down.*

HANS KARL

In our earlier conversation, I — up there in the small drawing-room —

HELEN

Ah, up there in the small drawing-room.

HANS KARL *made uncertain by her tone*

Yes, indeed, in the small drawing-room. I made a big mistake there, a very big mistake.

HELEN

Ah?

HANS KARL

I summoned up something that is past.

HELEN

Something that is past?

HANS KARL
Certain incongruous, purely personal matters which passed through my mind when I was out there in the field, and later in hospital. Purely personal imaginings. Hallucinations, as it were. Lots of things that were absolutely irrelevant.

HELEN
Yes, I understand you. And so?

HANS KARL
It was wrong of me.

HELEN
In what way?

HANS KARL
One can't summon up what's past, just like the police summons one to their station. The past is past. No one has the right to introduce this into a conversation which concerns the present. I'm expressing myself abominably, but my thoughts on the matter are quite clear.

HELEN
I hope so.

HANS KARL
I was much distressed in looking back, as soon as I was by myself again, feeling that at my age I ought to have myself better in hand — so I returned to give you back your full freedom (pardon me, the word sprang to mind in such a clumsy manner) — to give you back your full independence.

HELEN
My independence — to give it back?

HANS KARL *uncertain, is about to get up.*

HELEN *remains seated*
So that is what you wished to tell me — about your leaving earlier.

HANS KARL
Yes, about my leaving and, naturally, about my returning. The one determines the other of course.

HELEN
Aha. I'm very grateful to you. And now I shall tell you why you came back.

HANS KARL
You tell me?

HELEN *looking him full in the face*
You came back because — Yes! It does happen! God in heaven be praised! *She laughs*
But perhaps it is a pity that you came back. For this is not, perhaps, the proper place
for saying what has to be said — perhaps it might — but now it will just have to be
said here.

HANS KARL
Oh my God, you must find me inexplicable. Say it out aloud!

HELEN
I understand everything very well. I understand what drove you away and what it
was drew you back again.

HANS KARL
You understand everything? I don't understand it myself.

HELEN
We can speak more quietly, if it's all right with you. What drove you away here was
your distrust, your fear of your own self — are you angry?

HANS KARL
Of myself?

HELEN
Of your actual, deeper will. Yes, that's uncomfortable, that does not lead one along
the most pleasant route. It happened to lead you back here.

HANS KARL
I don't understand you, Helen.

HELEN *without looking at him*
Such goodbyes are not what is hard for you to bear, but what is sometimes hard, is
what goes on inside you when you are alone with yourself.

HANS KARL
You know all this?

HELEN
Because I know all this, I would have found the strength to do the impossible for
your sake.

HANS KARL
What impossible thing would you have done for me?

HELEN
I would have followed you.

HANS KARL
In what way "followed"? How do you mean?

HELEN

Through the door here and out into the street. I showed you my coat lying back there, didn't I?

HANS KARL

You would have — ? But where?

HELEN

To the Officers' Mess or elsewhere — who knows, until I had finally found you.

HANS KARL

Helen, you would have — ? You would have looked for me? Without even thinking that — ?

HELEN

Yes, without thinking of anything else. I'd follow you, Hans Karl — I only wish that you'd —

HANS KARL *with uncertainty in his voice*

You, Helen dear, you wish? *To himself* Here they are again, those impossible tears! *To her* I can barely hear you. You're speaking so softly.

HELEN

You hear me well enough. And these tears — but they even help a little to say what I —

HANS KARL

You — you were saying something?

HELEN

Your will, Hans Karl, your own self; please understand me. It turned you around when you were alone, and it brought you back to me, Hans Karl. And now —

HANS KARL

Now?

HELEN

Now I don't really know if you can truly love someone — but I am in love with you, and I want — but that really is beyond the pale, Count Bühl, that you should let me say this!

HANS KARL *trembling*

You want of me —

HELEN

Of your life, of your soul, Hans Karl, of everything — I want my share!

A short pause.

HANS KARL

Helen, everything you are saying here alarms me in the extreme for your sake; for your sake, Helen, purely for your sake! You are mistaken about me; I have an impossible character.

HELEN

You are as you are, and I wish to know you as you are.

HANS KARL

It's a dreadful risk for you to take.

HELEN *shakes her head.*

HANS KARL

I am a man who has nothing but misunderstandings on his conscience.

HELEN *smiling*

Yes, so it seems.

HANS KARL

I have hurt so many women.

HELEN

Love is not entirely sweet.

HANS KARL

I'm a boundless egoist.

HELEN

Oh yes? I don't believe it.

HANS KARL

I'm so unstable. Nothing can hold me fast.

HELEN

Yes, you can — how shall I say — be seduced and also seduce. You truly loved them all, and duly forsook them all. Poor women! They simply didn't have sufficient strength for you both.

HANS KARL

How so?

HELEN

To desire is your nature. But not just this, or just that, but rather — everything — and then for ever. One of them should have had the strength to compel you to desire ever more and more from her. You would then have stayed with her.

HANS KARL

How you know me!

HELEN
After a short while they all became indifferent to you, and you were madly sympathetic but felt no great friendship for any of them: that was my consolation.

HANS KARL
How you know it all, Helen!

HELEN
I lived only in that knowledge. That was the one thing I understood.

HANS KARL
Then I ought to be ashamed before you, Helen.

HELEN
Am I ashamed before you, then, Hans Karl? Oh no. Love cuts too deep into the flesh.

HANS KARL
All this you knew and endured —

HELEN
I wouldn't have stirred my little finger to remove such a woman from your side. It wouldn't have been worth the trouble.

HANS KARL
What kind of enchantment is it about you. Not at all like other women. You make one feel such inner calm.

HELEN
You can hardly conceive the friendship I feel for you. That will take a long time — if only you can give me that.

HANS KARL
How you say those words, Helen!

HELEN
Go now, Hans Karl, so that no one sees you. And come back soon. Come tomorrow, early in the afternoon. It concerns no one, but Papa ought to know soon. — Papa has to know, — he must! Or not, what do you say?

HANS KARL *embarrassed*
There is just — my good friend Poldo Altenwyl has for days had a little matter, a request — to saddle me with: he wishes — for no good reason, mind you, that I make a speech in the Upper House —

HELEN
Aha —

HANS KARL
And so I've been trying to avoid him for weeks to the best of my ability — avoid being left alone with him — in the Officers' Mess, on the street, wherever —

HELEN
Don't worry Dear — only the main thing is to be mentioned — that I guarantee. — Someone's coming: I must be off.

HANS KARL
Helen!

HELEN *already on her way, stops once more*
Dearest! God bless! *Takes up her coat and disappears through the little door to the left.*

SCENE NINE

CRESCENCE *above on the staircase*
Kari! *Quickly comes down the stairs* Have I finally found you! All this is quite simply confusion without end! *She sees his face* Kari! Something has happened! Tell me what!

HANS KARL
Something has happened to me, but we won't go into all that.

CRESCENCE
Please! Surely you're going to explain to me —

SCENE TEN

HECHINGEN *comes down from upstairs, stands still, calls to* HANS KARL *with lowered voice*
Kari, if I could just ask you over for a second!

HANS KARL
I'm at your disposal. *To* CRESCENCE Do please excuse me.

STANI *also comes down from above.*

CRESCENCE *to* HANS KARL
But what about the boy! Whatever shall I say to my boy? The lad is, after all, in an awkward position!

STANI *comes down; to* HECHINGEN
Pardon me a moment, simply must speak to my Uncle Kari! *Greets* HANS KARL.

HANS KARL
Forgive me just for a moment, my dear Ado! *Leaves* HECHINGEN *standing, steps over to* CRESCENCE Come over this way, but alone: I have to tell you something. But we won't, on any account, go to any lengths in talking it over.

CRESCENCE
But I'm not a person given to indiscretion!

HANS KARL
You are a perfect angel. So listen please! Helen has become engaged.

CRESCENCE
She has become engaged to Stani? She wants him?

HANS KARL
Do wait a bit! Don't get tears in your eyes at once; you still don't know.

CRESCENCE
It is you, Kari, you who make me feel so touched. The boy has you to thank for everything!

HANS KARL
Wait, Crescence! — Not to Stani!

CRESCENCE
Not to Stani? Well then to whom?

HANS KARL *with great embarrassment*
You can congratulate me!

CRESCENCE
To you?

HANS KARL
But now please be off, and don't bring it up in conversation. She has — I have — we have become engaged to one another.

CRESCENCE
You have! Well then, I'm delighted!

HANS KARL
I beg you now to remember above all, that you promised to spare me all this frightful confusion, to which anyone who goes about mixing with people is exposed.

CRESCENCE
I shall certainly do nothing — *with a glance towards* STANI

HANS KARL
I've told you that I wouldn't explain anything to anybody, and I must ask you to spare me certain misunderstandings.

CRESCENCE
Don't you get all suspicious now! You had the very same face on you as a little boy whenever you were thwarted. I couldn't bear it even at that time. Of course I'll do everything you wish.

HANS KARL
You are the very best woman in the world; but now you must excuse me, for Ado feels the need to hold conversation with me — that will now have to be absolved and have done with it. *He kisses her hand.*

CRESCENCE
I'll be waiting for you!

CRESCENCE *with* STANI *step to the side, at some remove but still visible from time to time.*

SCENE ELEVEN

HECHINGEN
You're looking at me so severely! There's a reproach in that glance!

HANS KARL
Oh, by no means: I do beg you not to judge my glances quite so finely today.

HECHINGEN
Has something occurred which has changed your opinion of me? Or your view of my situation?

HANS KARL *lost in thought*
Of your situation?

HECHINGEN
Of my situation in relation to Antoinette, of course! May I ask you what you think about my wife?

HANS KARL *nervously*
I beg your pardon, but I do not wish to say anything about women tonight. One cannot begin to analyse anything without falling prey to the most frightful misunderstandings. Therefore I ask to be exempted!

HECHINGEN
I understand. I fully appreciate it. From all that you say, or rather hint at in the most delicate way, there is only one conclusion for me to draw: that you consider my situation as hopeless.

SCENE TWELVE

HANS KARL *says nothing, looks disconcertedly to the right.* VINCENT *has stepped in from the right, wearing the same suit as in Act One, a small round hat in his hand.* CRESCENCE *has stepped over to* VINCENT.

HECHINGEN *most perturbed by* HANS KARL's *silence*
This is the critical moment in my life which I've seen coming. I need your support now, my dear Kari, if my entire world is not to be shaken to the roots.

HANS KARL
But my dear Ado — *under his breath, looking across at* VINCENT What's all that about?

HECHINGEN
I would like, if you'll permit, to recapitulate on the basic reasons which allowed me to hope —

HANS KARL
Excuse me for a second; I can see that some sort of confusion has arisen. *He goes across to* CRESCENCE *and* VINCENT.

HECHINGEN *remains on his own.*

STANI *has stepped back to one side with some signs of impatience.*

CRESCENCE *to Hans Karl*
Now he tells me: you're off at an early hour tomorrow morning — come now, what is the meaning of this?

HANS KARL
What does he say? I have given no instructions —

CRESCENCE
Kari, there's no end to all this shilly-shallying where you're concerned. Now that I've got into the mood for this whole engagement thing too!

HANS KARL
Would you mind —

CRESCENCE
Good Lord, it simply slipped out just like that!

HANS KARL *to Vincent*
Who sent you here? What does this mean?

VINCENT
Your Lordship surely gave orders himself, half an hour ago by telephone.

HANS KARL
To you? I never gave you any orders.

VINCENT
Your Lordship gave orders to the caretaker regarding departure tomorrow at seven a.m. for the shooting lodge at Gebhardtskirchen — or more precisely, this morning, since it's now twelve fifteen.

CRESCENCE
But Kari, what does all this mean?

HANS KARL
If I might be spared the trouble of rendering account for every breath that I take.

VINCENT *to* CRESCENCE
It's all quite easy to understand. The porter's wife ran upstairs with the message; Luke was not to be found at the time, so I took matters in hand. I notified the chauffeur, I had the suitcases brought down from the loft, I had Secretary Neugebauer woken up just in case he was needed — why should he be asleep when the whole house is up? — And now I've come here to be of service and to take further orders.

HANS KARL
Go back home at once; cancel the car, let the cases be unpacked again, ask Herr Neugebauer to go back to bed, and see to it that I never see your face again. You are no longer in my service; Luke is fully instructed for the rest. Dismiss!

VINCENT
Now that's a real big surprise! *Exit.*

SCENE THIRTEEN

CRESCENCE
Well, say just one little word to me! Just explain to me —

HANS KARL
There's nothing to explain. As I left the Mess I had, for certain reasons, made up my mind to leave on a trip tomorrow morning. That was at the corner between the Freyung and the Herrengasse. There's a café there which I entered, and I rang home from there; after that, as I stepped out of the coffee house, instead of turning off across the Freyung, as had been my intention — I walked down the Herrengasse and came back in here — and it was then that Helen — *he strokes his forehead.*

CRESCENCE
But of course I shan't bother you further. *She goes over to* STANI *who has sat down in the background.*

HANS KARL *pulls himself together and walks up to* HECHINGEN, *very sincerely*
I must ask you to forgive all that is past; I acted wrongly and misguidedly in every conceivable way, and I ask you to forgive me the error of my ways. I really cannot in detail give an account of this evening. I do ask you, nonetheless, to remember me with kindness. *Offers him his hand.*

HECHINGEN *dismayed*
But you're saying goodbye to me, old boy! You've got tears in your eyes. And I do understand you, Kari. You're a true, good friend; our sort just isn't capable of wriggling out of the fate which favour or disfavour with the ladies has in store for us; you, however, have raised yourself above this whole atmosphere once and for all —

HANS KARL *makes a gesture of denial.*

HECHINGEN
You can't deny it, there's a certain aura of superiority surrounding you: and just as everything in life consists ultimately of advancing and retiring, nothing stands still, so from day to day there gathers about you that ever-increasing solitude of the superior man.

HANS KARL
That's just another colossal misunderstanding! *He looks anxiously to the right where, in the doorway to the conservatory,* ALTENWYL *appears with one of his guests.*

HECHINGEN
How then? How am I to explain such words?

HANS KARL
My dear good Ado, I beg you to spare me the trouble of this or any other explanation. Let's move over there, please; there is something bound my way, to which I no longer feel equal today.

HECHINGEN
What then? What then?

HANS KARL
There in the doorway, there behind me!

HECHINGEN *looks that way*
But it's only our host, Poldo Altenwyl —

HANS KARL
— who considers this concluding point of his soiree the appropriate moment to stalk up to me with hideous intent; for why does one go to a soiree, but to allow anyone at all to collar you in the most merciless manner, with whatever appears important to him just then!

HECHINGEN
I don't follow —

HANS KARL
That the day after tomorrow, at a session of the Upper House, I am to make my maiden speech. He has taken this charming mission upon himself on behalf of our club, and since I keep avoiding them at the Mess and everywhere else, he now lies in

wait here in his house, for that second when I stand unprotected! I beg you to speak with me in an animated way, and with some agitation, as though we had something important to settle.

HECHINGEN
And you intend to refuse once again?

HANS KARL
I am supposed to stand up and make a speech on international reconciliation and on the coexistence of nations — I, a man convinced to the core of one thing in this world: that it's impossible to open your mouth without creating the most unholy forms of confusion! But I'd be better advised to rescind hereditary membership and to hide away in a hermit's den for the rest of my days. That I should fill my mouth with a torrent of words, each one of which seems to me actually indecent!

HECHINGEN
That's a wee bit strong as an expression.

HANS KARL *very heated, without being very loud*
But everything one utters is indecent. The simple fact that one utters something is indecent. And if you wish to be exact, my dear Ado (but then people just don't wish to be exact about anything on earth) there is something quite outrageous about even venturing to experience certain things! To experience certain things and not to sense that it's indecent in oneself, requires such towering self-adulation and a degree of blindness which, as an adult one might harbour secretly, but never admit to oneself. *Looks to the right* He's gone. *About to leave.*

ALTENWYL *is no longer to be seen.*

CRESCENCE *steps up to* KARL
Now don't you try and escape! You've simply got to talk the whole thing through with Stani now.

HANS KARL *looks at her.*

CRESCENCE
Now surely your're not just going to leave the boy standing there! My boy is showing such forbearance, such self-control, that I'm quite awe-struck. Surely you're going to say a word to him. *She beckons* STANI *to come closer.* STANI *comes a step closer.*

HANS KARL
All right, one final thing. But it's the last soiree you'll ever see me at. *To* STANI, *in approaching him* It was a mistake, my dear Stani, ever to entrust anything to my powers of persuasion. *Holds out his hand to him.*

CRESCENCE
Well embrace the boy! The boy has borne himself through all this business in simply peerless fashion.

HANS KARL *looks vacantly ahead, somewhat absent-minded.*

CRESCENCE
Well if you don't embrace him, then I have to embrace him for his brave bearing.

HANS KARL
Might I request this be done after I've left. *Gains the main exit briskly and disappears.*

SCENE FOURTEEN

CRESCENCE
Now it's all the same to me, but I must embrace somebody! Too much has taken place today for anybody with any heart, such as myself, just to drive home and go to bed without further ado!

STANI *takes a step back*
Well Mama! In my reckoning demonstrations fall into two categories. The one belongs strictly to the private sphere: to that I relegate all acts of tenderness between blood relations. The other has, so to speak, practical and social significance: it is the pantomimic expression of an extraordinary situation affecting family history, as it were.

CRESCENCE
Well, that's surely the one we're in!

ALTENWYL *with a few guests has appeared above and is on the point of descending the stairs.*

STANI
And for the latter, certain correct and accepted forms have obtained for a thousand years. What we have experienced here was, for better or worse, to call a spade a spade, an engagement. An engagement culminates in an embrace between the engaged couple. — In our case the engaged couple is too bizarre to adhere to these forms. Mama, you are the closest relative of Uncle Kari; there stands Poldo Altenwyl, the bride's father. Go up to him without another word and embrace him and the whole thing will assume its proper, official aspect.

ALTENWYL *has come down the stairs with some of the guests.* CRESCENCE *hurries towards* ALTENWYL *and embraces him. The guests stand there astonished.*

Curtain.

APPENDIX A

∼

The Irony Of Things

A long while before the war, I chanced upon this comment among the ' Fragments' of Novalis: "After a disastrous war, one ought to write comedies". This note, in its strangely laconic form, seemed rather baffling to me. Today I can understand it better. The element proper to comedy is irony, and indeed nothing is better fitted than a war which ends disastrously to clarify for us that irony which governs all things on earth. Tragedy bestows on its hero, the individual, an artificial dignity: it makes of him a demi-god and raises him above the circumstances of bourgeois existence. If it shifts but half a step away from this unconscious but necessary tradition, it slips into the realm of comedy. How close to the latter even a play like *Hamlet* comes — but Hamlet himself remains a king and a hero, though one whose very substance the irony of circumstances and self-irony already begin to act upon like rays of the sun on a snowman: and then a bourgeois tragedy is a wholly preposterous thing, for the bourgeois world is the world of the socially bound, while tragedy unfolds within what is socially boundless. Yet comedy proper sets its individuals in a thousandfold enmeshed relationship to the world, it sets everything in relation to everything else, and thus places everything in a relationship of irony. That is precisely how the war functions which overwhelmed us all, and which we have not yet escaped today, indeed may not escape for another twenty years. It set everything in relation to everything, the apparently great to the apparently little, that which apparently conditions things, to a new, higher principle by which in turn it is conditioned, the heroic to the mechanical, the emotive to the financial, and so on ad infinitum. At first, when the war began, the hero was ironized by the trench-digger; the man who wanted to stand erect and attack, by the man who wielded a shovel and dug in; at the same time, the individual was ironized by the mass to the point where his self-respect was crushed; indeed, not just the individual but the organized mass also, the battalion, the regiment, the corps, was ironized by the still greater and amorphous mass — that frightening and pitiable giant — by something intangible by which it felt controlled and impelled, and for which it is hard to find a name: let us call it the spirit of nations. Yet the moment came where these vast masses themselves, symbolically unified, were ironized by the momentary sway of certain individuals who had somehow got their hands on the levers of power by which this unwieldy whole could for the moment be governed. Yet at the same moment, they themselves were already subject to cross-currents of the most virulent, subversive irony: the irony of contrast within the great notional generalizations to which they paid lip-service when faced with that welter of stubborn facts with which they had to contend; the irony of the tool visavis the premature and wittingly untrue synthesis. And then the moment came when, within these gigantic composites, the concept of the nation was ironized by way of the concept of social class. The hour of coal and of the coal miner had struck: this entire complex of the apparently ideal behind which the essentially material hid, and the apparently material within which the ideal is imprisoned, and which we call European civilization; this was ironized by a single material substance — by sunlight stored in mineral form — and all social classes, even the working class, were again ironized by a given sector of this class: the coal miners, who stand in relation to this substance on which everything depends in a manner which again contains immense irony. For they are made to maintain a relationship to this very substance, which they have at their immediate disposal, not unlike that of slavery. In the struggle for the mind of the coal miner who was suddenly master of the situation, the social and national slogans became ironized in the extreme; indeed, since he was more closely bound to a landscape than another labourer, even those greatest of powers ironized themselves in their struggle over him, whose mutual irony on occasion flashes out through all this activity: geography and history. What finally became an inexhaustible source of irony is the circumstance that in all the conquered countries — that is in almost half of Europe — money lost its value against commodity, even the most modest commodity; a piece of bread or a length of linen, that it was now in fact impossible to purchase anything with that daemonic substance for which one was accustomed to give up everything blindly, because with it everything could once be bought; that over great stretches of the continent one had returned to exchange and barter, and that in the context of these changes, the privilege adhering to intellectual work had completely vanished and the head of a grammar school was paid more or less like a market labourer, and a State Secretary a little less than a chauffeur.

In all of this we find ourselves totally within the element of comedy — or rather, within an element of such universal irony as no comedy on earth displays, with the possible exception of Arisophanes; and that too arose during a war that proved most disastrous for the poet's native city and that sealed its fate. However, it is quite clear that it is the vanquished to whom this ironic might of events is made manifest. Whoever has come to the bitter end of any cause, will see the blindfold drop from his eyes; he will attain clarity of vision and gain deeper insight almost like one who has gone before.

The poets who were around a hundred years ago were sensitive to all these things, and quite naturally so; they had had to live through the upheaval in France and the Napoleonic era, just as we have to live through today's crises. For that reason, they created out of irony a fundamental ingredient of their vision of life and art and called it 'Romantic Irony'. They considered it wrong to immerse oneself too deeply in pain, and maintained that in order to love an object completely, one must also recognize the ridiculous aspect of such an object. They demanded that one consider the whole of life "a beautiful illusion born of genius", as "a marvellous theatrical spectacle", and whoever differed in approach lacked a proper sense of the universe. They rose above and beyond their times — once the great storm had passed and, as in our own day, the bitter and the shallow coalesced — to such great inner freedom that it might seem to us almost like intoxication. Today this cast of mind is easier for us to grasp than it could have been for any intervening generations, and we read with astonishment the words they wrote with a fiery flourish of the pen upon the dark, starless firmament: For our Master is Mind; and where Mind is Master, there Freedom is to be found.

(First published in: *Neue Freie Presse*, 27.3.1921)

APPENDIX B

Prussian and Austrian

An Outline

IN GENERAL

PRUSSIA:

Created, an artificial structure, by nature a poor country, everything within men and by men, hence: belief in the state as a cohesive force, more virtue, more efficiency.

AUSTRIA:

Grown, historical fabric, by nature a rich country, everything from without: nature and God, love of homeland as a cohesive force, more piety, more humanity.

SOCIAL STRUCTURE

PRUSSIA:

A loose social fabric, the classes divided by cultural differences; but precise machinery.

Lesser nobility strictly separate, unified in itself.

Homogenous officialdom:
Bearer of a *single* mentality.
"Governing" opinions and customs.

The people: a most readily disciplined mass, unlimited authority (army; scientific social democracy).

Supreme authority of the Crown.

AUSTRIA:

A tight social fabric, The classes united within the culture; the mechanics of the whole imprecise.

High nobility rich in types, politically disparate.

Polygenous officialdom:
No prescriptive way of thinking and feeling.

The people: independent mass, unlimited individualism.

Supreme confidence in the Crown.

THE INDIVIDUAL

PRUSSIA:	AUSTRIA:
Contemporary cast of mind (around 1800 cosmopolitan, around 1848 liberal, now Bismarckian, all but lacking recollection of past phases).	Traditional cast of mind, stable almost for centuries.
Lacking in historical sense.	Possesses historical instinct.
Strength in abstraction.	Little talent for abstraction.
Incomperable in orderly execution.	Quicker on the uptake.
Acts according to rule.	Acts according to fitness of things.
Strength in dialectics.	Rejects dialectics.
Greater skill in expression.	Greater sense of balance.
More logicality.	Greater ability to adapt to real life.
Self-reliance.	Self-irony.
Seemingly masculine.	Seemingly immature.
Transforms everything into function.	Bends everything round to the social.
Asserts and justifies himself.	Prefers to remain in the state of unclarity.
Self-righteous, presumptuous, school-masterly.	Bashful, vain, witty.
Driven towards crisis.	Evades crises.
Fights for justice.	Casualness.
Incapacity for empathy visavis others.	Empathy to the point of loss of character.
Willed character.	Play-acting.
Each individual bearer of a part of authority.	Each individual bearer of humanity as a whole.
Ambitiousness.	Hedonism.
Preponderance of the businesslike.	Preponderance of the private.
Fierce exaggeration.	Irony to the point of disintegration of self.

(First published in: *Vossische Zeitung*, 25.12.1917)

APPENDIX C

A Letter

This is the letter written by Philipp Lord Chandos, younger son of the Earl of Bath, to Francis Bacon, later Lord Verulam and Viscount St.Albans, being an apology to his friend for his total withdrawal from all literary activity.

It is most generous of you, my honoured friend, to overlook my total silence over two years and to write to me as you did.

It is more than generous of you to mark your concern about me, your perplexity at the mental torpor into which I appear to you to be declining, by an expression of levity and wit which only great men command such as are deeply versed in the perils of life and yet remain undaunted.

You close with the aphorism by Hippocrates: "Qui gravi morbo correpti dolores non sentiunt, iis mens aegrotat", and you say that I have no need of medication to conquer my affliction but, even more, to sharpen the sense of my inner condition. I wish to answer you in the manner you merit, wish to open my innermost self to you, yet do not know how I might bring this about. I scarcely know if I am still the same man to whom your precious letter is addressed; am I really that person, now twenty-six years of age, who at nineteen could lightly toss off the "New Paris", the "Dream of Daphne", the "Epithalamium"; all those pastoral plays dizzy with the delirious splendour of their diction, which a heaven-sent Queen and some all-too indulgent Lords and Gentlemen are still gracious enough to remember? Am I still the one who at twenty-three made the inward discovery of that complex of Latin periods beneath the stony arcades of the Great Square in Venice, whose mental blueprint and structure called forth greater inward rapture than any buildings rising from the sea by Palladio and Sansovino? And could I, if otherwise one and the same person, have so fully expunged from my inscrutable self all traces and scars of this issue of my most strenuous thought, that the title of the little tract named in your letter lying before me stares back at me as a thing cold and alien? So much so indeed, that I was unable to grasp it at once as a familiar pattern of organized words, but could only understand it word by word as though I had encountered these Latin terms, thus connected, for the very first time. However, I remain myself after all, and rhetoric underlies these questions; rhetoric which may suit women or the House of Commons, yet whose persuasive powers, so greatly overestimated in our age, cannot suffice to delve into the core of things. But I must disclose my innermost self to you; a peculiarity, a malaise, a malady of the mind possibly, if you are to grasp that I am divided by just such a bridgeless abyss from the literary tasks lying before me as from those which lie behind me and which I hesitate to call my property, so alien do they appear to me.

I do not know if I should more admire the intensity of your benevolence or the incredible sharpness of your memory when you once more recall for me the various little plans I carried about with me in those shared days of splendid enthusiasm. I truly had wished to depict the first years of the reign of Henry VIII, our deceased glorious sovereign! The posthumous memoirs of my grandfather, the Duke of Exeter, on his negotiations with France and Portugal offered me a sort of basis. And in those happy, active days there flowed into me from Sallust, as though through unstopped channels, that cognition of form, that deep, true, inner form which can only be surmised beyond the impediments of rhetorical artifice. Of such form it can no longer be said that it marshals the material, for it permeates it, renders it obsolete and creates poetry and truth at the same time; an interplay of eternal powers, something as magnificent as music and algebra. That was my dearest plan.

What is Man that he creates plans!

I also toyed with other plans. Your gracious letter conjures these up as well: each one sated with a drop of my blood, they dance before me like sad little gnats beside a gloomy wall on which the bright sunlight of those happy days no longer falls.

I wished to decipher the fables and mythical tales left to us by the ancients, and in which painters and sculptors take infinite, unreflecting pleasure as hieroglyphs of some secret, inexhaustible wisdom whose breath I believed I could sense as if through a veil.

I well recall this plan. Behind it lay I know not what sensuous and spiritual desire: like a hunted stag eager for the water I yearned to enter these naked, gleaming bodies, these sirens and dryads, this Narcissus and Proteus, Perseus and Actaeon. I desired to vanish into them and to speak out of them with tongues. I desired. There was so much else I desired. I thought of beginning a collection of 'Apothegms' such as Julius Caesar had penned: you will recall this cited in a letter by Cicero. Here I considered ranging side by side the most noteworthy expressions of thought which I could collect on journeys whilst in commerce with the learned men and sophisticated women of our day, or with certain members of the population or with educated and distinguished persons. I wished to unite with these, fine adages and reflexions from the works of the ancients and the Italians and whatever else I encountered of intellectual gems from books, manuscripts and conversations. Further to these: the arrangement of especially fine festivals and processions, remarkable crimes and cases of mental frenzy, the depiction of the greatest and most characteristic buildings in the Low Countries, in France and Italy and much else besides. The entire opus was then to be entitled 'nosce te ipsum' (know thyself).

To be brief: the whole of existence at that time appeared to me in a sort of enduring intoxication as one great unity. Spiritual and bodily reality seemed to me to constitute no contradiction, neither did courtly and animal life, art and non-art, solitude and society. In all things I felt nature, in the aberrations of insanity no less than in the extreme refinements of some Spanish ceremonial; in the gaucheness of young peasants no less than in the sweetest allegories. And in all of nature I felt my own self; when I drank deep draughts of foaming lukewarm milk in my hunting lodge, milked by a tousle-haired farm-hand from a mild-eyed cow's udder into a wooden pail, it felt no different from when I sat in the window-seat built into my study and drew in sweet foaming nourishment for the mind from a folio. One thing was like the other: nothing was of lesser degree either in its dreamlike unearthly nature or in bodily power. And so it continued through the entire breadth of life to right and left. Everywhere I stood in the midst of things and was never aware of mere semblance. Or then again, I instinctively sensed everything is a parable and every creature a key to the next, and I truly felt I possessed the power to grasp one after another by its antlers and to unlock with them as many of the others as could be unlocked. This will explain the title I had thought of giving that encyclopedic book.

It may appear as a well ordered plan by divine providence to one who has access to such beliefs, and that my mind must recoil from such swollen presumption into this utter fecklessness and impotence which remains my permanent inner state. Yet such religious concepts have no hold over me. They belong to the cobwebs through which my thoughts shoot into the void while so many of their fellows remain trapped there and come to rest. The mysteries of faith have hardened for me into a sublime allegory which extends over the fields of my life like a radiant rainbow set at a constant distance, ever prepared to recede should it occur to me to hasten there and to enfold myself in the hem of its mantle.

But, my honoured friend, earthly concepts also elude me in similar fashion. How shall I attempt to depict for you these strange mental torments, this swift upward jerk of fruit-laden boughs above my outstretched hands, this receding of murmuring waters before my parched lips?

My case is briefly, this: I have totally lost the capacity to think or to speak coherently about anything whatsoever.

At first it gradually became impossible for me to discuss a more demanding or general topic and thereby to have recourse to such words as are commonly and casually employed by everyone. I felt an inexplicable malaise in merely uttering the words 'mind', 'soul' or 'body'. I found it inwardly impossible to pronounce any judgement on the affairs at court, the events at parliament or whatever. And this was not because of any possible scruples, for you know my all but frivolous courage and frankness: but rather those abstract words which our tongue must of necessity employ to voice any sort of judgement fell apart in my mouth like putrid mushrooms. It so happened that I wished to rebuke my four-year-old daughter Katharina Pompilia for a childish lie of which she had been guilty and point out to her the need always to be truthful, whilst the terms which gushed to my mouth assumed such iridescent shades and so intermingled that I was scarcely able to stumble to the end of the sentence, just as if I had felt nausea. And indeed, with pallid face and pressure on my brow, I left the child standing alone, slammed the door behind me and only felt to some extent restored once on horseback and taking a brisk gallop across lonely pastures.

Gradually this infirmity spread like a corrosive rust. All judgements, even those in everyday domestic conversation normally made in carefree fashion and with unflinching certainty, became so dubious that I had to cease all participation in such conversations. I was filled with unaccountable anger, which could only be disguised with difficulty, to hear such things as: this affair ended well or badly for this or that person; Sherrif N. is a wicked, Preacher T. is a good man; Tenant M. is to be pitied, his sons are spendthrifts; another man is to be envied because his daughters are good housekeepers; this family is on the rise, another is in decline. All this seemed to me so unprovable, so mendacious, so full of holes as it is possible to be. My mind impelled me to see all the things which came up in such conversation as uncannily close at hand: just as I had once seen a piece of skin on my little finger through a magnifying-glass resembling a fallow field with furrows and hollows. That is how I now felt about people and their actions. I no longer succeeded in taking them in with the simplifying glance of habit. Everything disintegrated for me into parts, the parts into further parts, and there remained nothing that could be captured by a concept. Individual words swam about me; they assumed the aspect of eyes which stared at me and into which I in turn must stare. They are vortices which create vertigo when I look down into them, which spin relentlessly and through which one arrives at emptiness.

I made an effort to rescue myself from this condition and enter the intellectual sphere of the ancients. I avoided Plato, for I dreaded the perils of his metaphoric flight. I thought mostly of keeping faith with Seneca and Cicero. I hoped to recover health from this harmony of circumscribed and ordered concepts. But I was unable to make the transition to them. These concepts I understood well enough: I saw their wonderful interplay of relations rise up before me like magnificent fountains that played with golden orbs. I could hover about them and see how they interchanged in their play; but they were concerned only with each other and the deepest, the most personal part of my thinking remained excluded from their round dance. I was overcome by a feeling of terrible solitude in their midst. I felt as one locked into a garden with nothing but eyeless statues; once again I fled to free open spaces.

Since that time I lead an existence which I fear you will scarcely comprehend; it flows on so trivially, so thoughtlessly. It is an existence indeed scarcely to be distinguished from that of my neighbours, my relatives, and most of the landed gentry of this kingdom, and one not entirely lacking in cheerful and inspiring moments. I have some difficulty in suggesting to you wherein these good moments consist; here words let me down once again. For it is something totally nameless and, indeed, in all conscience scarcely nameable which at such moments intrudes on me, flooding some aspect of my daily surroundings like a vessel with its superabundance of higher existence. I cannot expect you to understand me without example and I must beg your indulgence for the paltriness of my examples. A watering can, a harrow abandoned in a field, a dog in the sunlight, a humble graveyard, a cripple, a little farmhouse; all this can become the vessel of my revelation. Each one of these objects and a thousand of their kind generally passed over by the eye with utter indifference, can suddenly, at some moment which is not in my power to command, assume for me a sublime and affecting character which lies beyond all words to express. Yes, it may even be the distinctly imagined idea of an absent object which is granted this mysterious privilege of being filled to the brim with that gently yet fast rising tide of

divine sensation. It so happened that I recently gave instructions to strew ample doses
of poison for the rats in the milk cellars of one of my dairy farms. I rode out towards
evening and, as you may imagine, thought no more about the matter.Then, whilst
riding at walking pace over the deeply furrowed field with nothing close by other than
a brood of quail put to flight, and in the distance the great sun setting over undulating
fields, there suddenly opened up within me this cellar, crammed with the death-
throes of that race of rats. Everything was within me: the cool musty cellar air filled
with the sickly pungent smell of the poison and the high-pitched death-screams
echoing from mouldering walls; those fiercely embroiled spasms of impotence, hectic
flights of criss-crossing despair; maddened search for escape; the cold look of rage
when two met at a blocked-off cranny. But what good is my searching for words again
which I have forsworn! Do you recall, my friend, that marvellous description from
Livy of the hours that precede the destruction of Alba Longa? How they stray through
the streets which they are never to see again … how they take leave of the stones on
the ground. I tell you, my friend, I carried this within me and the burning of Carthage
as well; but it was something beyond that, it was more divine, more bestial, and it was
the present; the fullest, most sublime present. There was a mother who had her dying
young in spasms about her and who directed her glances not at those who were dying,
not at the pitiless stone walls, but at the empty air, or through the air into infinity,
and accompanied these glances with a gnashing of teeth! — When a dutiful slave
stood close by the stiffening body of Niobe, filled with impotent terror, he must have
gone through what I went through, as within me this animal soul bared its teeth in
defiance of that monstrous fate.

You must forgive this description and should not think that it was pity which filled
me. You ought not to think that on any account, otherwise my example was clumsily
chosen. It was far more and far less than pity: a tremendous form of sympathy, an
outpouring of the self into these creatures or else a sensation that an effusion of life
and death, of dreaming and waking, had for a moment passed over into them — but
from where? For what had this to do with pity, what with intelligible human thought-
connection, if on yet another evening I find a half-filled watering-can beneath a nut
tree, left behind by a gardener's apprentice. The water in it is darkened by the shade
of the tree and a water-beetle scuttles across the surface of this water from one dark
shore to another; if this coincidence of trivia thrills me with such a powerful sense of
the infinite, thrills through me from the roots of my hair to the very marrow of my
heels, that I wish to break out in words which I know, were I to find them, would
draw to earth the very cherubim in whom I do not believe. Then I turn away in silence
from that spot and weeks later, when I catch a glimpse of that nut tree, I pass by with
a timid sidelong glance since I do not wish to dispel that lingering sense of the
marvellous which still haunts the stem, nor dispel the greater than earthly raptures
which continue to pulsate about the bushes close by. At such moments an
insignificant creature, a dog, a rat, a beetle, a withered apple tree, a cart-track snaking
over a hill, a moss-covered stone, means more to me than the loveliest, most adoring
lover in a blissful night had ever meant. These dumb and sometimes inanimate

creatures reach out towards me with such plenitude, such deep presence of love, that my fervent eye can scarcely find a spot that is dead. Everything, simply everything in existence, everything I recall, everything touched on by my most confused thoughts appears to me to have being. Even my own heaviness, the recurrent dullness of my brain, seem to hold significance; I feel a delightful, essentially infinite interplay of opposites within and about me, and among all the contending bodies there is none which I might not enter. It appears then as if my body consisted of endless ciphers which can unlock all things for me. Or it is as if we could enter upon a new, mysterious relationship with all existence once we had begun to think with our heart. Yet once this strange, trance-like state vanishes, I can give no real account of it; I am then no more capable of representing in rational terms what this whole world-embracing harmony consisted in and how it communicated itself to me, than I could give a precise account of the internal motions of my entrails or the stemming of the flow in my bloodstream.

Apart from these strange coincidences which, by the way, I scarcely know whether to attribute to mind or body, I live a life of almost unbelievable emptiness and have difficulty in disguising this inner paralysis from my wife and this indifference from members of my staff who remind me of the affairs involving the estate. The good, strict upbringing which I owe my father, and the early acquired habit of leaving no hour of the day unused are, it seems to me, the sole reason for preserving sufficient outward control over my life and the appearance appropriate to my standing and person.

I am rebuilding a wing of my house and can bring myself now and then to speak with the architect about the progress of his work; I manage my estates and my tenants and officials will likely find me somewhat more laconic but no less amiable than before. Not one among them standing in his doorway with doffed cap when I ride by in the evening will have an inkling that my glance, which he is wont to catch respectfully, is searching with silent longing beyond the decaying timbers under which he is used to search for angler's bait; my glance which plunges through the narrow, grated window into the stuffy chamber where the low bedstead with coloured linen in the corner ever seems to await someone who is to die or someone about to be born. Who is to know that my glance lingers on the ugly whelps or the cat which lithely slips through the flower-pots, and that amongst all these paltry and cumbersome objects of peasant life it is seeking for that unique thing whose inconspicuous form, whose wholly unremarked lying or leaning there, whose dumb essence may become the source of that mysterious, wordless, boundless rapture. For my unnamed feeling of bliss will sooner break forth from some distant, lonely shepherd's fire, than from the sight of the starry heavens, sooner from the chirp of a last dying cricket once the autumn wind drives wintry clouds across the empty fields, than from the majestic roll of an organ. At times I compare myself in thought with Crassus, that orator of whom it is reported that he grew so immeasurably fond of a tame moray, a dull, red-eyed, dumb fish in his ornamental pond, that it became the talk of the city. And when Domitius once reproached him before the Senate with having shed tears over this fish's death, and thereby attempted to make him appear halfway a fool, Crassus made him the reply: 'Then at the death of my fish, I did what you failed to do at the death of either your first or your second wife.'

I do not know how often this Crassus and his moray springs to mind as the mirror-image of my own self, bridging the abyss of centuries. But not on account of the reply he gave to Domitius. The reply brought the laughs over on his side so that the affair was resolved in a joke. Yet the affair touches me closely; this affair would have remained the same even if Domitius had wept tears of blood in sincerest grief for his wives. For Crassus would still stand confronting him with his tears for his moray. And it is on this figure, whose ludicrous banality amidst a world-governing Senate debating the loftiest issues is so glaringly apparent, on this figure some mysterious impulse compels me to reflect in a way that seems perfectly foolish, the instant I attempt to express it in words.

Sometimes the image of this Crassus lodges in my brain at night like a splinter about which everything festers, pulsates and boils. It seems then as if I myself were to ferment, to form blisters, to seethe and to sparkle. The whole thing is a kind of feverish thinking, but thinking within a material which is more immediate, more liquid, more glowing than words. They are equally vortices, yet not such as the vortices of language, which seem to lead into a bottomless void, but somehow into myself and into the deepest domain of peace.

I have pestered you unduly, my honoured friend, with this expansive depiction of an inexplicable condition which usually remains concealed within me.

You were so kind as to express your disappointment at the fact that no book published by me reaches you any more, 'to compensate you for the renouncement of my company'. At this moment I feel with a certainty, not unmixed with a measure of attendant pain, that I shall also not be writing a book in English or Latin within the coming year and in all the subsequent years of my life; and this for the sole reason that I leave this irksome aberration to your infinite intellectual superiority to establish its place without prejudice within your harmoniously ordered realm of spiritual and physical phenomena: and this because the language in which it might have been possible for me to write or think, is neither Latin, nor English, nor Italian and Spanish, but a language of which no single word is known to me, a language in which voiceless things speak to me and in which I may perhaps one day render account in my grave before an unknown judge. I wish it were given to me to compress into the last words of this in all probability last letter that I write to Francis Bacon, all the love and gratitude, the boundless admiration that I harbour in my heart for the greatest benefactor of my mind, for the foremost Englishman of my time, and will continue to harbour until it breaks in death.

D. 1603, this 22nd August.

Phi. Chandos

(First published in: *Der Tag*, 18/19 October 1902)

APPENDIX D

~

He and She

The cup she carried in her hand,
— Her chin and mouth reflect its round —
So light and steadfast was her tread,
No drop out of the cup was shed.

So light the sureness of his hand:
He rode upon a youthful horse,
And with a gesture, scorning force,
He brought it to a quivering stand.

And yet in reaching for the hand
Which would this light cup have bestowed,
The burden proved for both too great,
For both, in trembling, knew a state
Where neither hand its partner found,
And so to earth the dark wine flowed.

(First published in: *Wiener Allgemeine Zeitung*, 25.12.1896)

MHRA New Translations

The guiding principle of this series is to publish new translations into English of important works that have been hitherto imperfectly translated or that are entirely untranslated. The work to be translated or re-translated should be aesthetically or intellectually important. The proposal should cover such issues as copyright and, where relevant, an account of the faults of the previous translation/s; it should be accompanied by independent statements from two experts in the field attesting to the significance of the original work (in cases where this is not obvious) and to the desirability of a new or renewed translation.

Translations should be accompanied by a fairly substantial introduction and other, briefer, apparatus: a note on the translation; a select bibliography; a chronology of the author's life and works; and notes to the text.

Titles will be selected by members of the Editorial Board and edited by leading academics.

Alison Finch
General Editor

Editorial Board

For details of how to order please visit our website at:
www.translations.mhra.org.uk

Lightning Source UK Ltd.
Milton Keynes UK
UKOW04f0425290816

281677UK00001B/5/P